THE KINGDOM OF GOD

THE KINGDOM
OF GOD

D. Martyn Lloyd-Jones

Edited by Christopher Catherwood

CROSSWAY BOOKS
Cambridge

Cover photo: Cephas picture library

ISBN 0 85684 031 X

Production and Printing in England for
CROSSWAY BOOKS
Kingfisher House, 7 High Green, Great Shelford,
Cambridge CB2 1SG by
Nuprint Ltd, Station Road, Harpenden, Herts AL5 4SE.

CONTENTS

NOTE TO THE READER

These sermons were first preached in 1963. Normally all contemporary references are left out, in order to make sure that the sermons are timeless. However, that year there was a major scandal, often referred to as *the Profumo scandal*. (The Secretary of State for War, John Profumo, had an affair with a woman who was also involved with the Russian Military Attaché). The opprobrium heaped on Profumo was enormous. But the attitude of the Doctor was a model of Christian forgiveness, as is clear from Chapter 8, which we have therefore left as near to the original as possible. The sin was condemned, but the hope of salvation for repentant sinners comes through equally clearly.

As usual, the warmest thanks for all her hard work in checking my editing should go to Elizabeth Catherwood, the Doctor's elder daughter, who often does so much behind the scenes without any acknowledgement. Warm thanks should also go to Mrs Finney for retyping the manuscript and to Mrs Alison Walley for putting it on disk and for copy editing.

Christopher Catherwood, Editor

1 THE KING'S PROCLAMATION

Now after that John was put in prison, Jesus came into Galilee, preaching the gospel of the kingdom of God, And saying, The time is fulfilled, and the kingdom of God is at hand: repent ye, and believe the gospel (Mk 1:14–15).

THIS IS A MOST MOMENTOUS STATEMENT. In these words, this particular gospel-writer, Mark, gives us, at the very outset, an epitome, a kind of summary of the whole message that he is going to unfold in his Gospel. He has introduced it; he has given us very briefly, as is his character as a writer, certain essential preliminaries, but it is here he really comes to the thing that he wants to talk about. In a sense he announced it in the first verse by saying, "The beginning of the gospel of Jesus Christ, the Son of God." And then he went back and gave us a little glimpse of the ministry of John the Baptist who was our Lord's forerunner or herald. He was the one who came preparing the way for Him, calling people to be ready for Him and His message, saying that he was nothing but a voice himself, and that there was another mightier than he coming after him; one, "the latchet of whose shoes," he said, "I am not worthy to unloose" (Lk 3:16). "I," said John in effect, "am only preliminary; I am only preparatory; He is about to come."

Then Mark tells us here that John was cast into prison. This had happened to him because of his faithful preaching to king

Herod; his denunciation of the king's illegal marriage arrangements and life. John, therefore, was thrown into prison, and after that, Jesus came into Galilee and began His ministry. So I am calling your attention to this passage because it is such a perfect summary of Christianity and what it stands for and of what the message of the Gospel really is. And I do this, because there is, perhaps, nothing that is so sadly needed in this modern world as just to get a simple, direct, unvarnished statement as to what the Gospel is about.

Indeed, this is to me the standing and almost perpetual problem. How does it come to pass that, with open Bibles before them, men and women should be wrong not so much about certain details with respect to the Gospel, but about the whole thing, about the very essence of the Gospel? It is quite understandable that there should be certain points, certain facets of truth about which people are not clear and about which there may be division of opinion. This Gospel is many-sided, it has many aspects, so that is not surprising. But I do suggest that it is indeed very surprising that at the end of the twentieth century, men and women should still be all wrong about what the Gospel is; wrong about its foundation, wrong about its central message; wrong about its objective and wrong about the way in which one comes into relationship with it. And yet, that is the very position by which we are confronted at the present time.

Now I am not, in a way, blaming the modern man and woman, those who are outside the Christian Church. There is a sense in which I do not blame them for their bewilderment and for the fact that they are outside the Church, because, alas, we are living in days and times when the Church herself is mainly responsible for the confusion. So it is urgently important that at any rate we should be clear about our approach to this Gospel, because if our initial approach is wrong, everything else must be wrong. That is obvious, is it not? If you are setting out upon a journey; if you want to go to a given place, then you will not arrive at your destination if you set out upon the wrong road.

The time to be extremely careful is at the beginning, at the first step.

So, as I see it, the main trouble today with so many people who are quite honest and sincere, and who tell us honestly and sincerely that they are not Christians, is that their whole notion of Christianity is wrong and that therefore they must be wrong over all the details, as, indeed, they are.

Let me try to crystallise this by giving you a typical modern example of this very thing to which I am referring. A book called *Soundings* has recently been published, which has been written by a number of scholars in Cambridge. Now in his comments on the book, a reviewer makes a significant statement. First of all he quotes a sentence from the book: "It is a time for taking soundings, not charts and maps," and then he goes on to say, "If this suggests that the authors are all at sea, fair enough, so are we all or should be." That is how he views things and by "at sea" I think that what he really means is that we should all be somewhere on this unchartered ocean—that we should not be on the shore but on the sea!

But then he goes on, "The Church has no earthly chance of survival in the nuclear age if it thinks that the depths of the knowledge of God's truth are all known and can be plumbed by any one who sits at the end of the pier with a string of texts in his hand"—notice what he is saying there—"It is to be hoped that many of us will have the faith and courage to launch out into the deep with the authors of this book of pilot them."

There, I think, is a very representative statement of the modern position. To put it in other language, this is what the reviewer is saying:

"Now we must start from the point that you and I are living in the atomic age; that is the basic thing. We are living in 1963, not 1863, not 1763, not 1663, not AD 63. We are living in the atomic age and that has changed everything! What may have been true in the past is no longer so, and if the Church is to survive in this atomic age then you have got to give up this notion that truth is already known and that all the depths are already familiar to men. You must realise that you are out in the midst of an ocean; you have no map, no chart, you do not know where you are. The only thing you can do is to take soundings, to get some notion of the depth beneath you and of where you are. Are you near land or are you not? 'It is a time for taking soundings'!"

In other words, the whole position is that, because of the advance of knowledge, particularly scientific knowledge, everything is once more in the melting-pot, and all we can do now is to experiment, to try to make discoveries, to try, if possible, to get some sort of a map or a chart. But it is very difficult and it is no time for that, we are told. No, it is merely time for "taking soundings".

So there it is, what can men and women do? And the only thing they can do at this present time, in this atomic age, is, well, to begin to think again, to study, to read these great philosophers and scientists and try and get some glimpse of truth at least and to hold on to it as best they can. That is the way. And, says that reviewer, he hopes that many will have sufficient courage and faith to launch out into the deep with the authors of this book to pilot them. But how you can pilot without a chart and a map I do not know! I should have thought that a pilot is a man who knows the place, who knows the channel.

I once lived in a town where there was a dock and I used to notice two lots of men—indoor pilots and outdoor pilots. And when a ship had passed through the lock gates, the outdoor pilot came along; there was a bit of river to go down before you came to the sea. Why did they need this outdoor pilot? There is only one answer; it was because he knew the channel, he had it in his mind, he knew the map and he had a chart. He knew what to avoid; he knew when to keep near to this side, when to keep near to that; he knew, as the ship went out to sea, whether there were hidden sandbanks and so on. The value of the pilot is that he knows all this; he is an expert man. But here we are asked to venture out to sea, to be piloted by men who themselves tell us that they have neither chart nor map but that they are proposing to take some soundings!

Now that is the position in which so many find themselves today and it is because the words of our text seems to me to deal with that position and to answer it that I draw your attention to it. We are living, certainly, in a time of crisis, a time of confusion. We are living in a world in which a sudden disaster can happen to any one of us at any moment. If we could be sure and certain that we had got another fifty years to live, then you might say, "There is no need to be in a hurry about this. It's all very exciting, very thrilling; let's follow the investigation, let's take the soundings!" But, my dear friend, you and I may come to the end of the journey at any moment. Is there nothing that can be given us; is there no chart and compass; is there no knowledge; is there no pilot who can step on board and give me an assurance that I am going to arrive at the everlasting haven of God? That is what I want; is that not what you want? And, thank God there is a positive answer. I want us to consider these verses together, because I am not "taking soundings". I have a chart; I have a map and I want to tell you something about it as simply and as plainly as I can.

So let us look at how all this is dealt with here so clearly, and let us do so by considering the words that are used. "After that John was put in prison, Jesus came into Galilee, *preaching...*". There is the key at once. The word that is translated "preaching" here is a very interesting one and it is a word that is not confined to Christianity or to the Christian Church. It was very common in the Roman Empire at the time when these things were first written and when they first happened. It was a word that was particularly used in connection with the cult of emperor worship that had arisen. People did not always do that but a point came when they did begin to do so. We should not laugh at them because we have seen something very similar in this century with Hitler in Germany, and it has happened in other ways in other countries. Man is always ready to worship man, so let us be careful in our judgments.

So the word "preaching" came in this way. When a son and heir was born to the emperor, a proclamation was made, and the word that was used for that very process was the word translated "preaching". It was an announcement; it happened when the heir was born, when he came of age, and at his accession to the throne or to the imperial power. So what we are told here is that when John was put into prison, Jesus came into Galilee announcing, proclaiming, heralding. It was the particular work of the herald to do this very thing.

The word 'preaching' is interesting, therefore, because it at once conveys this notion and idea. A herald does not make an uncertain announcement, or get up and blow his trumpet and say, "Listen, we do not quite know what's happening nor what is going to take place, but, well, we only hope that something is going to happen!" That is not heralding! No, the herald has a definite specific message and that is why he gets up and blows his trumpet. "Listen," he says, "I've got something to tell you." Now that is the term that is used here about what our Lord did. It is the term that is used about what the apostles did afterwards, and it is the word that has been used about preaching in the Christian Church ever since.

So you see we start with a note of certainty, issued from the Imperial Palace. That was the first word uttered, not just a man getting up and saying, "Well, my opinion is that before long there will be an announcement." No! he stood up with a bit of paper in his hand and he said, "Issued by the Imperial Palace at such and such at time, we have the honour to inform you..." That is it—preaching. The very word carries with it the whole notion of authority, an absolute unequivocal statement.

Now this is the very opposite of inviting people to a quest or to a search. That idea has always been popular; this notion that a Christian is someone who is seeking and searching; someone who sets out on a journey into this vast unexplored expanse of truth. What is a Christian? "Well," people say, "Christians are men and women who do not just spend their time eating and drinking and indulging their passions. They are intelligent people and they set out in the search for truth and, oh, it is thrilling; it is wonderful! The unchartered ocean, the promised land, the unknown; and off you set, with this thrill and excitement on the quest for truth." This has always been very popular. People like the idea; it appeals to their spirit of adventure and there have been those who have not hesitated to say this. Their criticism of our evangelical gospel has always been that it is too certain and too dogmatic.

The poets like saying this sort of thing, do they not? They, of all people, have generally fooled themselves more than others— "To travel hopefully is better than to arrive!" says one of them. It sounds wonderful, doesn't it? The quest for truth, the excitement of the chase, the thrill of the investigation; how boring when you arrive! How disappointing when you really discover! You see, people who hold this view are not interested in truth at all; they are interested in themselves as seekers and searchers after the truth, and thus they fool themselves.

But life is not a game; it is not a play; it is not just playacting. Oh, life is serious and solemn; it is real and it is earnest. And that is the sort of life of the world that we find ourselves in today. So I thank God that as I look at this, I am not invited to some great experiment or to some great search or question or journey of exploration. In the midst of my failure in life, with my heart breaking and my soul bleeding, and as I am almost giving up in despair, I suddenly hear a bugle call or a trumpet sounding, and I say, What is that? And, thank God, I hear an authoritative proclamation; I hear a man saying, "Listen, I am a herald, I have a message from the Imperial Palace; I announce to you." "Preaching"!—and that is the beginning of the Gospel.

But let me translate that into simpler, more ordinary language. My task is to tell you that the answer to all your questions is in this one book, the Bible. If I am a herald (and, thank God, unworthy though I am, that is what I am) I am not here to tell you my theories and my ideas about life, for they are no better than yours. No, I have been given a message from the Imperial Palace and here it is. And I am here to tell you with authority, with the authority of God, that all your questions have already been answered and all your problems have already been solved. You have but to listen to this preaching, this proclamation, and you will find peace and rest for your soul.

And if you should be asked to pass from time to eternity today, you will know where you are going; you will not be alone; you will be able to say with the Apostle Paul, "I know whom I have believed, and am persuaded that he is able to keep that which I have committed unto him against that day" (2 Tim 1:12). Thank God for preaching—proclamation, authoritative pronouncement!

So there is our first word; now let us go on to the second thing which we notice about this Gospel, about this Christian preaching. It is that it announces a plan and a purpose. "Where do you find that?" asks someone. Well, look at verse 14: "Jesus came into Galilee, preaching the gospel of the kingdom of God, And saying, The time is fulfilled." Which means that the time that has been spoken of has now come to pass. What is this "time"? Now here is the great message of the Bible, from beginning to end. It is, simply, that God has a plan and a purpose for this world of sin and of shame.

Here we are, in our failure, in our unhappiness, in our utter confusion. We have tried, we have striven, we have done our best, but it comes to nothing. The world gets worse and worse and so do we, and we get more and more hopeless and more filled with despair. We are baffled by the immensity of the problems, and all this scientific discovery makes it worse rather than better, so here we are in a condition of utter hopelessness. We have tried to read the philosophers but they do not know any more than we do. They can speculate, and make their dogmatic assertions, but we find that they are disproved, they are always being changed. What do we do, where can we go; is there any hope of deliverance; is there any possible way out?

And here comes the message: there is such a way. God had a plan and a purpose for this world and it is a plan to deliver men and women such as ourselves out of the morass into which we have fallen. To give us, in the midst of this unchartered ocean, a map, a chart, a compass, a direction, a pilot, everything we need. God Himself has planned it. Now all that is implicit in this phrase "the time is fulfilled"; the time of God's plan coming, as it were, into operation has actually arrived.

The Bible puts it like this. It says that God had made this plan even before the foundation of the world itself. The Apostle Paul says in 1 Corinthians 2:7, "We speak the wisdom of God in a mystery, even the hidden wisdom, which God ordained before the world unto our glory." That is it. That is the essence of this proclamation that is being made; the essence of Christian preaching. It does not say to us, "Well now, there is truth in that unchartered ocean, get out on to it; take your soundings, try to get your bearings, try to find out. Yes, you have discovered a little bit! You may go for weeks and find nothing; months, years pass, then just another little glimmer. At last…ah, it won't happen in your time, it will happen perhaps, well, in your grandchildren's; it may perhaps be even longer than that, but go on, it is marvellous, keep on. Keep on searching. You will find that you have been wrong, as your forefathers were, but go on seeking!"

No! Christian preaching is the exact opposite to that. The message of the Bible is not to urge us to try to find truth; it is to ask us to listen to the truth, to God's truth. For its whole point is to say that God, knowing Himself, knowing man, knowing everything, has devised and schemed a plan whereby men and women can be delivered out of their failure and sin and can be made citizens and worthy citizens of God's kingdom. God's plan!

But it not only tells us that God has a plan and that He planned it before the foundation of the world, it tells us also that God has made this plan known. We read in Hebrews: "God, who at sundry times and in divers manner spake in time past unto the fathers by the prophets, Hath in these last days spoken unto us by his Son" (Heb 1:1–2). The Old Testament is nothing but God revealing His plan and His purpose and He did it in that extraordinary way. He took a man called Abraham and turned him into a nation, and then He spoke to that nation. He gave them His word, which was then collected; they called them "the oracles of God" and we call them "the Old Testament". He took a man called Moses and gave him a revelation of how He had created the world and man; how sin had come in and what had happened, and how He had this great plan and purpose which He had worked out. God has revealed it all, and the message of the Bible is just to tell us about this plan and purpose of His, which He has revealed in that way through the instrument of men, in order that we may know what we must do and find salvation through it.

Then, the next thing that follows is that this is something that God has already done; and because He has already done it I need not waste a second in trying to discover truth. All I need to do is to pay attention to the truth that God has already revealed through the prophets, through the teachers of the Old Testament, through His Son, through the apostles of the New Testament. It is all here. I do not need anything fresh or new; all I need has already been given.

And, of course, that is why preaching is possible. If it were anything else it would not be preaching, it would be a sort of philosophical or a semi-political ethical society, and I would be saying, "Well now, we see the mess we are in, what can we do?" And I would put theories and ideas before you and say, "What do you think about it? Shall we try it; shall we see how we get on with it?" You see, it has nothing to do with this message. Here is a proclamation which comes and says, "Thus saith the Lord," or, in effect, "This is my way, this is my plan; believe this and you will find that it is true." That is the message, God's plan; nothing matters but this.

And, of course, in the light of that, all this talk about "the atomic age" is just stuff and nonsense—it has nothing to do with it! Why? Because God is still what He was two thousand years ago. God does not change; the splitting of the atom does not make the slightest difference to Him. God's character is what He has always revealed it to be; He revealed it through Moses in the Ten Commandments. He is a holy God; He is a hater of sin and He will punish it. God will never change—He is "the Father of lights, with whom is no variableness, neither shadow of turning" (Jas 1:17). I will go further. God *cannot* change; it is impossible. He is from everlasting to everlasting.

He is the eternal absolute God, the all and in all. "I am everlastingly—I am what I am."

But, at the same time, it is equally true to say that man does not change. "The Church," says that reviewer, "has no hope in this atomic age." Why not? Well, they say, "because men and women are now different; they know things that they did not know a hundred years ago." Do they? All right! of course they know that they can split the atom. Even I, when I did some science[1], was taught that there was nothing smaller than the atom, and that the atom is indivisible. That is wrong, of course, now! We were told it then with great dogmatism, but by now that is wrong, and probably what they are saying now will be wrong in about a hundred years or so! I do not know, and it does not matter; all I am concerned to say is this: What has all that got to do with me? Are people as people any different? Are they different morally; have they given up drinking because they have split the atom; have they given up immorality because they can send men and women up into outer space; have they ceased to have lusts and passions and evil desires within them because of all these tremendous advances?

The answer, of course, is that these things do not make the slightest difference at all, they are of complete irrelevance. The problem of men and women today is what the problem has always been. The problem has been this from the beginning: There were two brothers, one called Cain, one called Abel. And Cain was jealous of Abel and murdered him! People are still like that. Read about the characters in the Old Testament, and you will find them there. They are drunkards, adulterers and thieves, full of jealousy, envy, malice, spite, greed and avarice. It is all still with us. These are the problems of life; the atom has nothing to do with it. The problem is man, man as a moral being; and all these other things do not touch it.

And so we must get rid of this notion that because we are in the atomic age we need something new; we do not. You remember how that reviewer put it. He said, "You get rid of this notion that you can sit at the end of the pier with a string of texts in your hands. Don't believe," he said, "that ultimate truth is already known." He continued—and this is the thing that is monstrous—"the Church has no earthly chance of survival in the nuclear age if it thinks that the depths of the knowledge of God's truth are already known." But they are all known! They have all been revealed by God Himself. If the knowledge of God were dependent upon people seeking and searching, then obviously one generation would have an advantage over the previous one; but as we happen to be in the position in which by searching we cannot find God at any age or at any time, then we are entirely dependent upon His revelation. And as God has already given His revelation, the people to whom it first came knew as much as you and I know and nobody will ever know more than they did.

Now this is absolutely crucial and basic. You see, according to that other argument, you and I should know more about God than the Apostle Paul did; we should know more about the Lord Jesus Christ than the apostles did. Why? Because we are in the twentieth century, in the atomic age, and look at the great aggregate of knowledge that we have obtained since! But according to this it makes not the slightest difference, none at all! The Christian Church is built "upon the foundation of the apostles and prophets" (Eph 2:20). Why is this? It is because God chose these men, these apostles and prophets, to give them the revelation; to give the knowledge that men and women need. They were special people. In that old dispensation, He had these men whom He called prophets. He took them, He chose them and when He had taken a man He gave him a message and then He guided him and inspired him by the Spirit in the careful accurate writing and recording of it. God did it all. Now the man was not a passive amanuensis; no, his personality comes in, but the message and the truth of it is entirely from God, not man. It is the same with the apostles. And if the world lasts another billion years, men and women will never know more about God or about Christ or about heaven or about hell or about salvation, than they can know now if they read the Bible with spiritual eyes.

We are in no more advantageous position than the people of

the first century. Who would like to say that any modern man knows Christ as well as Paul knew Him? What arrogance it is, indeed, what nonsense it is. This is not a matter of knowledge adding to itself; this is receiving the revelation that God gives, and He has given it once and for ever.

The next thing that we are told about it, therefore, is that this plan of God is carried out by God acting in history. This again is a vital point. Christianity is not primarily teaching, it is a recorded history. Christianity is not urging men to think and to try to delve into the mystery and to discover the truth about God. It says, "Listen, this is what God has done." Is that not what happened on the day of Pentecost at Jerusalem? Is that not what the people said about the apostles when they began to speak with other tongues? What is this? they said, "We do hear them speaking in our tongues"—what?—"the wonderful works of God?" (Acts 2:11). Not the thoughts of God but the works of God, the things that God has done.

And that is the message of Christianity. Here it is: "Now after that John was put in prison"; that is a fact of history, an event in time, just as Julius Caesar landed in Britain in 55 BC. So, at a given point in time, John the Baptist was thrown into prison, and at that moment "Jesus came into Galilee, preaching the gospel of the kingdom of God, and saying, The time is fulfilled." "Listen to me," He said, "It has happened, it has come." Now what does this mean? It means that your salvation and mine depends not upon our thoughts, nor upon our discovery of truth, but entirely and utterly upon something that has literally happened in this world almost two thousand years ago.

So we preach to this atomic age and this is what we say; not "Come and join us on the unchartered ocean and help us to take soundings in order that we may arrive ultimately." No, we say, "Look back, look back; go back two thousand years, to the first century, listen: 'When John was thrown into prison Jesus came and said…'." That is it. In other words, our salvation depends not upon our understanding but upon what God has done in Christ.

Thank God for this! We are not all philosophers. We have

not got great brains and understandings but when we are told a fact we can believe it. There is a man standing and saying, "I have come from the Imperial Palace; a son and heir has been born to the Emperor." I am no philosopher but I can understand that! "Good!" I say, "Wonderful! I should like to see that Child." So here comes a proclamation which says, "When the fulness of the time was come, God sent forth his Son, made of a woman" (Gal 4:4), and it means your salvation if you accept it and give yourself to it. It is a unique event.

There is a further reason for us never to talk again about "this atomic age". No "age" makes any difference at all, because the turning point of history was two thousand years ago. Here is the crucial event of all time, the unique event, God's event, God acting. Here it is: "When John...Jesus came." History! the only age that matters is that point, the new dispensation, God's time.

So the preaching of the Gospel comes to us and it does not invite us to a quest or to an endeavour or to some wonderful thrill of hoping to find it. It says, "Just as you are, look back. God has already done all that is necessary for your every need and for your salvation." And what is that? It is that which is called here a "gospel"—He came "preaching the gospel of the kingdom of God, And saying, The time is fulfilled, and the kingdom of God is at hand." That is not a good translation; a better one is: "The time is fulfilled and the kingdom of God has drawn near." He does not mean that it is about to come. He says it has come; it has drawn, or come, near. Indeed, "It has arrived," he says, "amongst you."

Now what our Lord was saying was this: "God," He says in effect, "as you know, has been promising throughout the centuries that He is going to do something crucial. Read your Old Testament, remember what God said away back in the Garden of Eden. He said, 'It is all right, you have sinned and you will be punished but the seed of the woman shall bruise the serpent's head.'" That is it. It is going to come, and on through the Old Testament this promise is repeated; it is coming and all the prophets were looking forward to it.

Look at Isaiah 40:1: "Comfort ye, comfort ye my people, saith your God." He said it eight centuries before Christ was born, but what he was saying was this: "All flesh shall see the salvation of God." You do not see it now, said the prophet, but "Every valley shall be exalted and every mountain and hill shall be made low." Prepare a highway, be ready, this Messiah, this deliverer; He is coming! And all the prophets said the same and the people were waiting and longing for him.

And then our Lord suddenly appeared and began to preach, and He said, "The time is fulfilled and the kingdom of God has come." What God has promised throughout the centuries, He has now fulfilled. "This," said our Lord, "is good news, this is Gospel." Why? Well, because it is an announcement of the King, of the kingdom of God. He preached "the kingdom of God". And the kingdom of God means the reign of God. The world is as it is because it has rebelled against Him and men and women are in their present trouble and distress because they are rebels and because they are reaping the fruits of their own evil deeds, and God is pouring His punishment down upon them.

Take it from me, my friend, "the way of transgressors is hard" (Prov 13:15); "There is no peace saith my God to the wicked" (Is 57:21). And your clever modern men and women in the atomic age are in trouble, and as long as they turn their backs upon God their trouble will increase. But the kingdom of God is the very antithesis of that. It is the rule of God, it is the reign of God. It means the coming of righteousness, the coming of peace. It means that evil is controlled and defeated; it means that God's blessings are showered upon the Christian. It means that we bask in the sunshine of God's favour. It means that we become heirs of God and with a hope of everlasting bliss. That is what it is. One of our hymns puts it very well—

> Hark the glad sound! the Saviour comes,
> The Saviour promised long:

This is preaching—

> Let every heart prepare a throne
> And every voice a song.

Why?

> He comes, the prisoners to release
> In Satan's bondage held;
> The gates of brass before Him burst,
> The iron fetters yield.

Men and women are slaves to sin; they are in misery and bondage and unhappiness and they cannot break free. Here comes the One who can break the bars of iron and the gates of brass asunder; He can set the prisoner free!

> He comes, from thickest films of vice
> To clear the mental ray,
> And on the eyeballs of the blind
> To pour celestial day.

> He comes, the broken heart to bind,
> The bleeding soul to cure,
> And with the treasures of His grace
> To enrich the humble poor.
>
> Philip Doddridge

That is what is meant by "the kingdom of God".

Our Lord, back in His home town at Nazareth, went, as was His custom, into the synagogue on the sabbath day. They handed the book to Him and He began to read, and this is what He read: "The Spirit of the Lord is upon me, because he hath anointed me to preach the gospel to the poor"—not to the philosophers, nor to the great men of the atomic age, but to the poor of all ages— "He hath sent me to heal the broken-hearted, to preach deliverance to the captives, and recovering of sight to the blind, to set at liberty them that are bruised, To preach the acceptable year of the Lord. And he closed the book, and he gave it again to the minister, and sat down. And the eyes of all them that were in the synagogue were fastened on him. And he began to say unto them"—notice this—"This day is this scripture fulfilled in your ears" (Lk 4:18–21). He said, "The kingdom of God has arrived; God's favour has come. The day of release, the day of pardon, the day of renewal, the day of new life, the day of rejoicing in God and His government instead of rebelling against Him; it has come, the day of the favour of the Almighty, the day of grace has drawn near, it has arrived. Good News!"

Oh yes, and especially when you consider how it has arrived. It has come, you see, in this Person—"the beginning of the gospel *of Jesus Christ.*" "Now after that John was put in prison, Jesus came into Galilee, preaching the gospel of the kingdom of God." So the gospel of Jesus Christ is the same as the gospel of the kingdom of God. It is in the coming of this Person that the kingdom of God has come. God has been saying throughout the centuries, "I am going to send a Deliverer." Now He has arrived; but where has He arrived? In the stable in Bethlehem, there He is, a little baby in the manger. He is the one who is King; the Kingdom comes with the King. He has arrived and here he is preaching. Who is he? He is the Son of God; "The beginning of the gospel of Christ, the Son of God" (Mk 1:1).

This is the Gospel. You and I are not left to try to delve into the mystery of the being and the person of God and to try to discover a way out of our predicament. No, the message is this: God "hath visited and redeemed his people" (Lk 1:68). "God so loved the world"—this world, this damned, foolish, evil world that you and I live in and of which we are all a part by nature—God so loved it, "that he gave his only begotten Son, that whosoever believeth in him should not perish, but have everlasting life" (Jn 3:16).

Forget about the atomic age! Look back; look at the Babe in the manger, there He is—God in the flesh, God's Deliverer, God come down to deliver you, to rescue you. He does so in His Person, in His teaching and in His work—Mark goes on to tell us all about it in his Gospel. And He does it supremely by dying upon a Cross on a hill called Calvary. That is the crucial act, because you and I, as we are, cannot enter into the kingdom of God; we are rebels, we are sinful, we are guilty, we are vile. You cannot live in God's kingdom unless you are a worthy citizen.

How, then, can I enter? He is the answer. This is the Good News, that He bore our sins "in his own body on the tree, that we being dead to sins, should live unto righteousness" (1 Pet 2:24). Here is the message: "God was in Christ, reconciling the world unto himself, not imputing their trespasses unto them...for he hath made him to be sin for us, who knew no sin; that we might be made the righteousness of God in him (2 Cor 5:19,21). And thereby by dying on the Cross, He has opened the gateway into the kingdom and He says, "Today is the day of salvation, enter in."—"Come unto me all ye that are weary and heavy laden and I will give you rest" (Mt 11:28).

"The time is fulfilled"; the time promised so long ago has arrived, the kingdom of God has drawn near, has come. He says, "I am the King; come unto me just as you are." Thank God you do not have to put yourself right first; you do not have to understand the profundity first; you do not have to set out on some great quest. You may have to die very soon and your question is: "How can I stand before God; how can I know that I am going to heaven and eternal bliss?"

And this is the answer: "The time is fulfilled, the Kingdom has come"; the King is the Lord Jesus Christ and He loved you so much that he died for you and your sins, and all He says to you is, "Repent, think again, believe my message." Repent and believe the Gospel, acknowledge your folly and your sin, acknowledge your shame and your helplessness. Stop making enquiries, stop setting out with your great intellect to understand. Say, "I can't, I fail; God is God and I am human, finite, sinful; I cannot. I believe that you are the Son of God and the Saviour of my soul." That is all, simply believe—

> Only believe, and thou shalt see
> That Christ is all in all to thee.
>   John Monsell

My dear friend, don't be a fool! You do not understand life; you do not understand death; you do not understand yourself. You know nothing about tomorrow, how can you understand

God? Give up; give in. Believe on the Lord Jesus Christ and you will be saved as the Philippian jailer was saved by believing it (Acts 16); as men and women have been saved by believing it throughout the centuries ever since. Believe on the Lord Jesus Christ now; believe that this is God's plan that He sent His only begotten Son into the world to redeem us because He alone could do it, because He alone was mighty enough to take our sins and bear the punishment, and, nevertheless, to come out on the other side and rise and take His seat at the right hand of the Majesty on High.

"Believe on the Lord Jesus Christ and thou shalt be saved" (Acts 16:31). Is that good news to you? That is the test, you see. Are you thrilled by it; do you really want to sing about it? Do you want to

> Crown Him with many crowns,
>   The Lamb upon His throne;
> Hark! how the heavenly anthem drowns
>   All music but its own.
>   Awake, my soul, and sing
>   Of Him who died for thee,
> And hail him as thy chosen King
>   Through all eternity.
>   Matthew Bridges/Godfrey Thring

Do you want to do that? If you do not, it means that you are so blinded by sin and by Satan that you do not know that you are a lost soul; that you do not know that if you die like that, you go to hell, to everlasting misery.

But if you have ever seen your need and failure, if you are afraid to die and to face God, as anyone in their senses must be, then, you say, "This is the most wonderful news I have ever heard, that God sent His own Son to reconcile me unto Himself. And in my utter helplessness and hopelessness all I do is to cast my sins on Him, cast myself on Him, cling to Him just as I am." There is nothing like it in heaven or in earth; it is the most glorious Good News that has ever come. That and that alone is the message of the Christian Gospel. Repent, if you have never done it before, and believe the Gospel and be saved. You will be saved. Whether you die soon or not will be an irrelevance; nothing matters, you will be right, reconciled to God, with your eternal future absolutely safe.

---

[1] Dr Lloyd-Jones was a medical doctor.

2 THE FIRST PRIORITY

> But seek ye first the kingdom of God, and his
> righteousness; and all these things shall be added unto
> you (Mt 6:33).

I N THOSE WORDS OUR LORD BRINGS to a head all the
various things that He has been putting before His disciples and others who were listening to Him as He preached
what we know as "The Sermon on the Mount". What He is
concerned to do here is to give a general view and picture of His
kingdom, and of what He had come into the world to do. At
the very beginning of His ministry, He wants to make it plain
and clear to the people what He is proposing to do, and so He
preaches this sermon and He takes up various matters in it. But
ever and again during the course of the sermon, He makes one
of these general statements in which He sums up the whole
position, the entire teaching.

So the verse we shall consider now is an example and an
illustration of that very thing. Here, as it were, in a single verse,
we have the essence of the Christian message, the Christian
Gospel; and I want to try to show you how, in this one
statement, all its essential characteristics are put before us and
are emphasised for us. And this becomes particularly true of it
when we take it in its setting and in its context.

My reason for calling your attention to this is, again, that I
am anxious that we should all be perfectly clear as to the nature

of the Gospel. We looked in the last chapter at a similar statement—the announcement of the beginning of the ministry of our Lord Himself—and we considered that for the same reason. We saw that He, the King, made His great proclamation concerning the kingdom. And we saw, too, that certain essential aspects of His ministry and His teaching were stated clearly before us.

So we are looking at the similar statement here in this verse because of the tragic and terrible confusion that is so obvious at the present time with regard to what Christianity really is. There is this utter confusion, men and women are bewildered and, as I have said, I have a great deal of sympathy with them in their bewilderment. If one took one's notion of Christianity from the newspapers and certain popular books, one could end in nothing but confusion.

But, thank God, we need not turn to such sources for our information; we have here these authentic gospels, these documents produced by the early Church. Indeed, we know nothing about our Lord apart from what we are told here; all else is mere conjecture, mere imagination and supposition. There is only one thing to do; we must go back and discover what it was that the first preachers preached and we must go right back to the Lord Jesus Christ himself. And here, in this Sermon on the Mount, He puts before us in a clear and unmistakable manner what are obviously the bare essentials of His message and of His proclamation.

Now, as we look at this statement, we shall see that, there are certain general points which strike one at once, and then there are certain particular emphases which are also equally evident. The first general point is, surely, that this Gospel, this message of the Lord Jesus Christ is something which is altogether and entirely different from everything that has appeared before it; different from everything that men and women think of instinctively and believe by nature. The Gospel seems to come in the first instance, therefore, as a challenge to us and as a condemnation of what we have habitually believed.

Our Lord, you notice, puts it like this. He says in verse 31:

"Therefore take no thought, saying, What shall we eat? or, What shall we drink? or, Wherewithal shall we be clothed?", and then in verse 32, "(For after all these things do the Gentiles seek:)". Now we must remember that He was preaching to Jews, to people who had got their Old Testament Scriptures, who regarded themselves as the people of God and who were concerned about God and about righteousness. And the division of the ancient world to them was, of course, Jews and Gentiles; those who had got this religion and those who had not.

And that is an equally appropriate classification in our day and age and generation. "The Gentiles" are those who do not know the revelation; they are people who trust to their own thoughts and their own ideas, who live as if God has never been pleased to reveal anything at all concerning Himself. So the division is as appropriate now as it ever has been; and the point I am making is that our Lord emphasises the great fact that what He teaches is altogether different from the view of the Gentiles. It is altogether different from everything that has ever been thought by man or conjured up in man's mind or imagination.

This, again, is a very important preliminary point which we must never lose sight of. The Christian position, the Christian way of life, is not only slightly different from every other, it is essentially different; it is something that stands out alone and unique and apart.

But let me put that, secondly, in this way. To say that is another way of saying that, according to this teaching, the trouble with men and women as they are by nature, and the cause of their troubled world and all their ills and problems and vexations, the cause of all that is not something superficial; it is something which is very deep and very radical and very profound. And I emphasise that because of the very words our Lord uses: "Seek ye first." Where is your emphasis, he says; what is the first thing? In other words, He is concerned with first principles.

Now there are many people who seem to think that the criticism which Christianity makes of the natural man—man as he is by nature, the human philosopher and thinker—is that they are just wrong at certain particular points; that they are defective here and need a little bit more there, but that there is nothing radical. So many people think that the difference between Christians and non-Christians is that Christians are a little bit better than others; they have added on certain things; and stopped doing others, but that there is no profound, no essential change taking place. But, according to this teaching, that is of course, a complete and utter fallacy.

Notice the words that our Lord constantly uses. We have already considered "first", but there is another one and that is "the heart". He says in verse 21, "Where your treasure is, there will your heart be also." In other words, He says in effect, "The difference between my teaching and the other teachings is that it is one that applies to the heart." Now the heart is the very centre of life and of being, so it is not just something on the surface, it is, rather, something in the deepest, the most central part of man.

And then, in order to make it still more clear, He uses the analogy and illustration about the eye. He says, "The light of the body is the eye: if therefore thine eye be single, thy whole body shall be full of light. But if thine eye be evil, thy whole body shall be full of darkness. If therefore the light that is in thee be darkness, how great is that darkness!" (vs 22,23). He is concerned, you see, about the eye and again, this is a central organ, through which light enters into every part of the body. In other words, He says that the trouble is not in some little finger or in some odd portion of the body; no, it is right in the centre.

This is clearly a most important principle therefore. Christianity says that the trouble with men and women is in their heart, in their ultimate power of vision and understanding. It is not that they are partially wrong, they are all wrong; they are looking in the wrong direction, they are blinded at the most vital point. The organ that keeps them going, is itself in trouble—the heart. So our Lord puts this great emphasis upon "first", and "heart", and "eye" and this is just a pictorial way of saying that what the human race needs is not just to be improved a little bit here and there. That has been the fatal fallacy, surely, of the last hundred years in particular; it is the fatal fallacy of all those who think that by social or political enactments the world can be put in order.

But that is the exact opposite of this teaching. Here is a teaching which says that man's trouble is much too deep for that, it is too radical, too profound. Men and women do not need to be patched up; they do not just need a coat of varnish or a little improvement here and there; they need to be radically changed. Man needs to be new from the depths, from the foundations, from his very rudiments. And that, of course, is just another way of putting the great New Testament doctrine which says, "You must be born again" (Jn 3:7).

And so the third general point which our Lord makes is this. He calls us to a great act of committal. "Seek ye first." He means by this that it is not just a point of view, it is not just something to be argued about; Christianity is a way of life. And it is a way of life that demands a total committal, it is, if you like, a totalitarian demand. It does not merely ask that we consider it and say, "Oh yes, I can take on that teaching; that's a good emphasis there, I'll add that!" No, it is not something to be applied as we think and when and where. He says, "Seek ye first."

In other words, let me put it like this. Men and women will never know the truth of Christianity or the blessings that it can given, until they have given themselves to it. You can examine Christianity from the outside, but you will never know it, you will never get it. "If any man will do his will," says our Lord, "he shall know of the doctrine whether it be of God" (Jn 7:17). Here is a great fundamental principle about this way of life— "Taste and see that the Lord is good" (Ps 34:8). You will never know that the Lord is good until you have tasted Him, until you have tried Him. So many of us are like a man standing in an orchard, and there he looks at an apple tree or a pear tree and he examines it at a distance. Somebody says, "You know that's got a most wonderful flavour. If only you would try it, you would say that it is the most wonderful fruit you've ever tasted in your life." But the man looks on and he is not quite satisfied; he is not convinced and he can argue and stay there for as long as he likes, but he will never know, until he takes it and puts it in his mouth and bites it and proves it. "Taste and see that the Lord is good."

A theoretical examination of Christianity will never bring us anywhere. Our Lord always calls for a committal. "If any man," He says, "will come after me, let him deny himself, and take up his cross, and follow me" (Mt 16:24). That was His great expression: "Follow me"; you will find it running right through the pages of the four gospels. So it is a way of life to which we must commit ourselves, to which we abandon ourselves; listening to this blessed speaker who stands before us.

There, then, are the three main general characteristics of this message, and it is very important that we should always bear them in our minds. Unless we are clear about these things there is little point in proceeding. This is something that has come from heaven. Our Lord's claim is that He is the Son of God, and that He is the fulfilment of all the prophecies. "The time is fulfilled, and the kingdom of God is at hand," it has come, it has arrived. That is His claim. He says, "I am absolutely unique, listen to me, come after me." And it is something that no one had thought of, that no one would ever have imagined; it cuts right across all our ideas. It is something which is entirely apart.

So let us see how our Lord works out those three general principles in a particular and detailed manner, for that is what He does in this statement.

The first thing He tells us, therefore, in detail, is that all man's troubles are due to the fact that he has a false view of life. Why is the world in trouble? Why is it as it is today? Why are we all what we are? Why is everyone in the world not perfectly happy and at ease and contented and enjoying life to the full? What is the matter? Nobody will dispute the proposition that this world is a world of sorrow, of pain, and of unhappiness. But why? That is the first question, surely.

And our Lord's answer is quite simple. He says it is all due to the fact that men and women, as they are by nature, have a false view of life. That is the trouble, He says, with "the Gentiles". The Gentiles were living a terrible kind of life. There are many descriptions given of it in the pages of the New Testament, particularly in the epistles, and you will find hints of it also in the Acts of the Apostles. But why were they living like that? Well, the answer is "as a man thinks so he does."

You see, it is our view of life that determines how we live, and if our view of life is wrong, then, obviously, everything else will be wrong. "If the light that is in thee be darkness, how great is that darkness" (v 23). If the lens, the focus, is wrong what can be right? Everything is controlled by the eye in this matter of light, and if the eye is not single, if it is double or if there are opacities then, clearly, everything that passes through is going to be affected by it.

That is our Lord's teaching; and He says that the whole tragedy of the world is that its view of life is altogether wrong; that men and women, by nature, always put the wrong things first. We always proclaim what we are by our priorities. It does not matter what people say; all their protestations and everything else are of very little value. It is what people do in practice, what they really do in action that tells us exactly what they believe. It is their order of priorities that matters. You can work that out for yourselves but we all know how perfectly true it is. What are the things we hold on to; what are the things we shed first?

Now there are endless illustrations of this. Look at it, for example, in terms of people who go to Church. I am not saying this by way of criticism; I just put it as a way in which we can conveniently test ourselves. We are put off from attending the House of God by various things, are we not? But would we be put off in the same way by the same things from going to a theatre or a cinema? That is how you test your priorities. And our priorities proclaim our point of view.

So, then, according to our Lord the trouble with people is that they put the wrong things first, and that is why the world is not Christian today; that is why most people never attend a place of worship. They think they know what they need; they think they know what makes life and what makes for happiness. And so they think that all they have to do is to attend to them and that then all will be well!

So what are those needs, what are their priorities? Well, our Lord has listed them for us and they are as true today as they were two thousand years ago. "Lay not up for yourselves treasures upon earth" He says (Mt 6:19); but that is what man does, what he has always done. Money! Money is almost invariably one of the chief priorities with men and women because they believe that if you only have money why, then you can get anything! Money is power! People who have money are those who will be in control; and those who have money can buy whatever they want. They can buy happiness, they can buy anything—money! And, our Lord says, that is how the Gentiles are living— "Laying up for themselves treasures upon earth" and, He goes on, "Where your treasure is there will your heart be also" (v 21). There is no question about it.

What are their other priorities? In verse 25, He talks about food and drink. The world spends a great deal of its time in considering this. "I say unto you, Take no thought for your life what ye shall eat, or what ye shall drink: nor yet for your body, what ye shall put on." But, again, that is what men and women are doing and they keep on talking about it, and so He comes back to it and says, "Therefore take no thought, saying, What shall we eat? or, What shall we drink? or, Wherewithal shall we be clothed?" (v 31). These are people's priorities, says our Lord, and to them the big thing in life is: "What am I going to eat and drink? I can't be happy unless I eat and, of course, unless I drink." Look at the thousands of people in the world tonight whose happiness depends entirely and solely upon food and drink, and especially drink!

And then, there is this matter of clothing. "What shall we put on; how shall we appear before people?" The way to be happy is to impress people with your beauty or your greatness or this or that; your elegance! And immediately, everybody looks at you with admiration, so you are perfectly happy and you put your head on your pillow at night with great content-ment; you have achieved your objective. Money, food, drink, clothing, these are the things, says our Lord, for which people live.

In other words, you see, He says that the tragedy of life is due to the fact that men and women are living and are thinking as if they were only bodies. The thought, the attention, the planning, the scheming, the thinking, all go in the realm of the body; they conceive of themselves as if they were but animals. That is what animals do, they eat and they drink and so on; and so do men and women. These are the things they talk about, and, as you see a peacock preening himself so does a man and so does a woman. What I put on, the impression I make! They live for these things, says our Lord, and hence all the troubles.

And, of course, there is this other priority which He men-tions, and that is the extension of your life in this world. He puts it in these words: "Which of you by taking thought can add one cubit to his stature?" (v 27). What that really means is, "Which of you by taking thought can add one inch, as it were, to your duration of life?" But that is what people are interested in; to prolong life, and all the care, and the thought and the attention that they put into that! I am not saying that this is wrong. Certainly thank God for medicine; thank God for the cure of diseases; thank God for the extension of life; but, says our Lord, do you make that your priority? Is that the thing that you are living for; are you thinking of life in terms of existence only?

Now that, He says, is what the Gentiles do. And there is no doubt at all but that that is what constitutes life to the vast majority of men and women in our country today. Their happi-ness depends upon the amount of money they have, food, drink, clothing, extension of life; this is happiness, this is life; they do not think about anything else. But according to our Lord this is all wrong. It is wrong, first of all, because it always leads to slavery. He puts it like this: "No man can serve two masters"—you cannot, in other words, be a slave to two mas-ters at the same time—"for either he will hate the one, and love the other; or else he will hold to the one, and despise the other. Ye cannot serve God and mammon" (v 24).

Here is where the Gospel always comes in as a sword; for it says it is either the one or the other. The Gospel does not condemn money root and branch, let us make no mistake about that. A man is to be a steward and he can use money in a right way. There is nothing wrong in money in and of itself, but what is condemned is that a man should serve it, that he should live for it, that he should be mastered by it, that it should govern his whole outlook and that he becomes its slave—You cannot serve God and mammon.

But the fact of the matter with that view of life is that it always leads to slavery. And the world is living in slavery today. The desire for money, the power of money! The slavery of the social round, eating and drinking and clothing, what a horrible slavery it is! Now, this is not just my idea; you can read about it in the medical journals. There is a great problem in the United States of America at the present time over this very thing. They call it "the suburban disease", or, "the suburban complex". They talk about the strain on the suburban women in America, keeping up with their neighbours in food and drink and house and clothing and motor car; it is getting them down and it is creating a psychological problem. Now that is slavery; and the teaching of the Bible from the beginning to the end is that if men and women give themselves to these things they always become their slave; they are governed and mastered by them. They are no longer free, they are dominated; their whole life is determined by them.

But then our Lord mentions something else that such an attitude leads to. It is a part of the slavery, of course, and that is that it always leads to anxiety, to worry and to fear. That is what He is talking about when He says, "Take no thought for your life" (v 25). He means, "Do not have an anxious care." The translation is not quite as good as it should be here. "Take no thought" means, "don't be worried, don't be anxious, don't have an anxiety complex"—"Take no thought for your life, what ye shall eat, or what ye shall drink; nor yet for your body, what ye shall put on. Is not the life more than meat, and the body than raiment? Behold the fowls of the air...". Why are you so anxious about all this? asks our Lord.

Then again: "Why take ye thought for raiment? Consider the lilies of the field" (v 28). Our Lord's whole teaching here is a repetition of His earlier "Take no thought"; do not be anxious and burdened; do not be worried. But people who live for things like that always are anxious; they always are worried and full of fear. They are anxious that they are not as good as somebody else or that they have not got as much as somebody else. They are afraid that they are going to lose what they have got. Do you know there are many people in this world today who, if they lost their money, would be done for. If they could not buy their pleasure; if they had to sell their house; if they had to go without their car; if they could not dress well any longer, they would be finished! Everything they lived for would have gone and they are fearful and anxious and apprehensive. Is a war coming; am I going to lose my health? and so on. They live in a constant condition of fear and dread.

That is why this is the age of phenobarbitone and the tranquillisers. It is supposed to be the affluent age, I know, but it is at the same time the age of anxiety, the age of strain, the age of frayed nerves, the age of the complexes. It is inevitable. The modern age is proving the rightness of our Lord's teaching. You cannot live for these things; you cannot have these things as your priorities without becoming their slaves, and the slavery will show itself in the strain, the anxiety, the worry, the fear.

These things never really satisfy, they never really leave one at ease. "Uneasy lies the head that wears a crown," said Shakespeare. Yes, it is perfectly true. You are not safe, there are always others trying to get at you. I was reading (again in a medical journal) about big business and the strain on the men at the top. It has reached a point at which they cannot trust anybody else; they are afraid that all these others are manipulating, waiting for the opportunity to strike. So if you live for these things, if you are governed by ambition and by your own ideas of life along this line, then—"Uneasy lies the head."

There is never rest nor peace; there is never any ultimate satisfaction.

There then is our first heading. Man's troubles are all due to the fact that he has a wrong view of life; he has got the wrong priorities. So it follows in the second place that man's first and chiefest need is to get a right and a true view of life. Here it is: "Seek ye first..." and it is introduced with the word "But". "Don't do that," our Lord says, "*but* seek first." So here is the right view, here are the true priorities. And this emphasis is not only central to our Lord's own teaching, this is the great teaching throughout the Bible. So, what are the priorities; what are the things I should be thinking of, instead of food and drink and money and clothing and all these other things? Let us look at them.

"Oh, stop thinking about yourself," says our Lord in effect. What is man? Is he just an animal, a creature that is in this world to eat and to drink? "Take no thought for your life, what ye shall eat, or what ye shall drink; nor yet for your body, what ye shall put on. Is not the life more than meat, and the body than raiment?" Life! that is what I ought to think about. Before I give myself to the world's view of life and its priorities, I should start by saying, "Wait a minute; what am I? Am I only an animal?" "No," says our Lord, there is something bigger in you than your body and that is your life; and life is not the same as existence. There is that within men and women which is called the "soul". They are not in this world merely to eat and to drink and to buy their pleasures with their money and to cut a figure on the stage of life and to get the acclamation of others. No, they have a soul; they belong to eternity, they are made in the image of God. That is where you begin.

You must start by just asking yourself that first question. What is man? The Bible tells you away back in the book of Genesis, "Let us make man in our own image" (Gen 1:26). The lord of creation, a creature endowed with reason and great faculties and propensities, a reflection of the almighty God. He is not just a creature, he is not like the animals, he is lord of the animals, he is distinct, he is apart. That is man, so you can no longer put as your priorities eating, drinking and the things that can be bought with money, and your clothing. No, no, there is something in me unseen and hidden—" 'Dust thou art, to dust thou returnest' was not spoken of the soul," saith Longfellow. There is that within me which cries out for something bigger, vaster; that is the thing to start with.

But then, our Lord adds to that something which is infinitely more important. And that is men and women in their relationship to God and His Kingdom—"seek ye first the kingdom of God, and his righteousness." That is to be your priority. What does He mean by this? Well, I realise that I am bigger than my body, bigger than the world in which I find myself, bigger than lusts, instincts and desires—I myself. I have a sense within me that there is a power outside me. Everybody born has this sense; it is there in the most primitive races, a belief in a supreme high God; a sense that there is Another, the Unknown God that those Athenians were worshipping nearly two thousand years ago (Acts 17:23). There it is—God.

Begin to think about God our Lord. Why? Because God is the creator, the maker and the sustainer of everything. It is God, He says, who has made the birds of the air: "Consider"— "behold the fowls of the air: for they sow not, neither do they reap, nor gather into barns; yet your heavenly Father feedeth them" (v 26). This is great doctrine about God as the sustainer of the cosmos and as the great provider, the God of providence in His eternal might and glory.

But modern men and women do not think about God, they are not concerned—"What shall I eat; what shall I drink; wherewithal shall I be clothed? The pleasures I can get and the money." What fools they are, because the whole time they are ignoring and neglecting this God—because man cannot do without a God—they make gods for themselves. They worship food, drink, clothing, themselves, their own achievements, possessions, money. They worship, they serve mammon. Human beings are always worshippers and here they are, in their folly, worshipping false gods of their own creation and in the meantime they are not worshipping God, the God who made the fowls of the air, the lilies and the beauty of the flower and the form and the design, and all the magic and the marvel of it all. And they never give Him a thought! Oh, this is madness! says our Lord.

Get right in your thinking about yourself, then think of yourself in your relationship to God. And the moment you do so, He says, you will realise that you are utterly dependent upon Him, because the animals are, everything is. "It is he that hath made us, and not we ourselves" (Ps 100:3); our times and our breath are in His hand. God brought us into being and He could end it in a moment; we, none of us, control life; God controls it all. But men and women do not stop and think about that. They say, "What shall I put on tonight; how shall I dress tomorrow?"; and they may be dead before tomorrow! But they do not think of that. The whole of life, for them, is without God, He does not enter into their calculations.

That is why the world is as it is says our Lord. If only all men and women believed in God they would all humble themselves before Him. If only the whole world believed in God there would be no preparation for war, there would be no jealousy and envy and rivalry, because all men and women would be bowing before Him and worshipping Him and living to His glory and His praise. But because they do not, they set themselves up, they are the gods and they worship themselves and there is a rival god. So there are barriers between nations "I am going to be bigger," says one, so he makes a bigger bomb. "I will make a bigger!" says the other. And up, and up, and up we go and we get worse— "Whence come wars and fightings among you? Come they not hence, even of your own lusts...Ye ask and receive not," says the apostle James (4:1,3). You will never satisfy your god and so, according to the Bible, we get all the troubles in the world, individual troubles and collective troubles; national troubles and international troubles! It is all this rivalry because we are not living as under the eye of an almighty God.

So we have seen the meaning of "Seek ye first"; and "the kingdom of God", what does that mean? It means the rule of

God, the reign of God. It means that God, after all, is not only the maker of this world and its controller, He is also its governor. And how vital it is that we should begin to discover something about His rule and His reign—"the kingdom of God and his righteousness." And by that our Lord means that God is just and holy; He is righteous; "God is light and in Him is no darkness at all" (1 Jn 1:5). God is perfect in all His ways. He made a perfect world and He meant it to be perfect but it has gone wrong. But God does not change and He is going to put this world right; He will bring in His Kingdom. That is what Christ said: "The kingdom of God is at hand," it has come, the time is fulfilled, I am bringing it in, I am bringing it near and it is a kingdom of righteousness.

This means that, whether we like it or not, we are all under the eye of God, and we are all under His government. He is able to bless us in a manner that passes our comprehension and baffles our description. So why are we not experiencing these blessings? If is because God only blesses those who are righteous. God curses the rebel—"the wrath of God is revealed from heaven upon all ungodliness and unrighteousness of men" (Rom 1:18). Read your Bible, read the Old Testament and you will see that repeatedly. God blesses those who serve Him, who submit themselves to Him, and who are righteous in His sight.

This is the first thing to discover says Christ—"the kingdom of God and his righteousness." His kingdom is coming; He sent His Son into the world in order to establish it and to found it; He is gathering men and women into it and a day is coming when this Son of God will return again and He will finally judge the whole world in righteousness. He will destroy His enemies, all who have not submitted to Him, all who are not righteous; and they will go to "everlasting destruction from the presence of the Lord" (2 Thess 1:9).

"The kingdom of God and his righteousness." There is no room for evil in the kingdom of God and there will be none. When the kingdom of God has fully and finally come in the person of the Lord Jesus Christ, evil will be utterly banished, there will be nothing left, and all who belong to it will go to perdition with it; there will be nobody left except the righteous. "Then shall the righteous" says Christ, "shine forth as the sun in the kingdom of their father" (Mt 13:42); but only the righteous, they alone will be blessed.

So then, what our Lord says is this: These should be your priorities. "Seek ye first the kingdom of God and his righteousness"; realise that because you are a man or a woman you are a responsible being; that you are living your life under God, that your food and your drink will vanish, and that your clothing will not matter. You will not be interested in them when you are facing death and you may be in that position at any moment. Food, drink, clothing; if you offer them to someone who is dying, to somebody who is desperately ill, they are not interested! "Well," says our Lord, "live your life like that, realise that nothing matters except your relationship to God and that He is a righteous and a holy God; that He is the Judge of the whole world and that He will establish His kingdom." Listen to Christ; here He is, the Son of God and He says, "I have come to tell you that I am introducing and inaugurating it. Get into my kingdom, flee from the wrath to come; repent, believe the Gospel." Why? Because you cannot evade the righteousness of God and the coming kingdom and reign of God over the whole world.

These are the true priorities. This is what Christianity is about. No other teaching is saying this in the world today and that is why I emphasised at the beginning that it is unique and absolutely different. The world will encourage you to go on eating, drinking, putting on your clothing, trying to extend your life in this world. No, no, says Christianity. Life is full of uncertainties, you never know what the morrow will bring forth. "It is all right," says our Lord in effect, "don't worry about that, get right with God, believe in Him; enter His kingdom, the 'kingdom of God and his righteousness', and then you have got your right priorities."

So the next question is: How are these to be obtained? How can I know that I am in the kingdom of God; how can I be righteous; how can I be in a position that God will bless me?

"Seek it" says Christ; put it first, put everything else on one side; do not read another book, do not look at another film until you are certain of this. Do not do anything until you are certain of this; seek it first; be urgent about it—"Strive to enter in at the strait gate" (Lk 13:24). Strive with all your might and main to be righteous in the sight of God. Is it not obvious? Is this not sheer logic?

But you will not have tried for very long before you realise that it is an utter impossibility. At first you pull yourself up and say, "I am not an animal, I have a soul and not merely a body, and I see that God is holy and that I must be holy. God and unholiness cannot dwell together; light and darkness cannot be mixed; I must be perfect, I must cease to sin. I must live a godly and a holy life." So you begin to do it, but the more you try the blacker you see yourself. You develop a new sensitiveness that you never had before. You have a new discrimination and you feel you are vile, your thoughts are evil and you cannot do anything and there you are, hopeless; you feel lost and damned.

But it does not matter, go on. Seek, and go on seeking, until you are absolutely desperate and frantic and do not know what to do with yourself. And then come back and listen to this blessed Person again. He said to you at the beginning, "Seek ye first the kingdom of God and his righteousness," and He says, "All will be well if you do that." And you have set out and you have tried to do it and you feel further away than you were at the beginning. So go back to Him, and you will hear His voice, as you turn round, saying to you, "Come unto me all ye that labour, and are heavy laden and I will give you rest" (Mt 11:28). Carrying your awful load of sin, carrying the blackness of your own unregenerate heart, striving and all in vain, listen to Him: "Take my yoke upon you and learn of me, for I am meek and lowly of heart and ye shall find rest unto your souls" (Mt 11:29).

"Come to me," He says, "in your desperation. You are trying to make yourself righteous; quite right, it is the obvious thing to do if you want to be in God and His everlasting kingdom but you cannot do it, and you are realising that.

Listen," He says, "I came into the world from heaven in order to give you the righteousness that you can never achieve for yourself. That is what I am here for. I had to urge you to seek it, because I had to awaken you. You had got the wrong view, you had got the wrong priorities. You have got the right ones now and you see the utter impossibility of doing anything about it yourself. But I have come into the world; I have lived the law for you; I have satisfied every demand of God's holy law for you. I bore your punishment in my body on Calvary's Cross. Your sins are forgiven, your righteousness is abolished, it is washed away and vanquished in my blood. Come let me clothe you with the robe of my own righteousness."

That is what He will tell you. But He only says that to people who really seek Him; He only says that to those who are desperate about this and their souls and their salvation. Have you sought righteousness; have you sought to enter the kingdom of God? Oh, get up and seek it, go after it as Martin Luther did. But if you give up everything, become a monk, fast, sweat, pray, put on a camel-hair shirt and do all that the saints have tried to do, you will find that it will lead you nowhere. But you are quite right in your trying, and your seeking. If you never ask, you will never receive; if you do not seek, you will never find; if you do not knock, it shall never be opened unto you. But if you do seek you will hear Him and His gracious invitation, and He will say to you, "Listen to me, come after me. 'Whosoever will come after me, let him deny himself, and take up his cross and follow me' (Mt 8:34). Come wherever I lead you, leaving everything if necessary, leave every thought and consideration, simply follow me."

So that is what He says, and what is the result? Well, you notice, "Seek ye first the kingdom of God and his righteousness—and all these things shall be added to you." And what He means is that if you seek the kingdom of God and His righteousness; if you believe on the Lord Jesus Christ as the Son of God and your Saviour and the giver to you of righteousness, then you will get immediate soul satisfaction. It will be the end of your vain and useless striving, and you will indeed find rest and peace for your soul. You will know that all your sins are forgiven, "though they be as scarlet, they shall be as white as snow" (Is 1:18); though you have sinned into the deepest depths of hell, they are all forgiven in the blood of Christ and you will know it. What a knowledge! Peace with God—"Being justified by faith we have peace with God through our Lord Jesus Christ" (Rom 5:1).

But not only that—through whom or "by whom also we have access into this grace wherein we stand" (Rom 5:2). This means that you are given the knowledge that you are not only forgiven but also that you become a child of God; that you are indeed a citizen of the blessed kingdom of God with all its righteousness; that God is no longer your judge, He is your Father and He loves you with a Father's love. He has counted the very hairs of your head, they are all numbered; there is nothing He will not give you and He will begin to shower His blessings upon you.

But one of the most wonderful aspects of all to me about this verse is this. It means that now you have a very different view of "these things". Before, you lived to eat and to drink and to dress and now, oh, you still eat and you drink, and you still dress, but you do not live for them; you do it just because they are essential to life and no more. Your desires are so greatly reduced, and you are given them all, more than you want. You are not interested, you have a superfluity of them now and you are ready to give them to others. You lived for them once but now you say, "Oh, what does that matter?" You have a new view of life and you are now more anxious to know God than anything else. You do not care if you are a pauper as long as you are a child of God. You do not want to be in the highest circles of society; you are happy to be with the lowliest in the land if they are only Christians and can talk to you about Christian things. You will say with the writer of the hymn—

> Man may trouble and distress me,
> 'Twill but drive me to Thy breast;

Life with trials hard may press me,
Heaven will give me sweetest rest.
Henry Francis Lyte

It does not matter; once men and women have entered into the kingdom of God and have received the righteousness in Jesus Christ, their whole view of life has changed. This old world has now become a pilgrimage to them through which they have to go. They see it as a world of ugliness because of man's sin and rebellion against God; they do not say, "Isn't life marvellous and thrilling." 'Oh," they say, "how terrible is 'man's inhumanity to man.' Man is the creature of lust and passion and vice and evil and ugliness." Yes, life is a vale of tears, but they must go through it and they are ready to go through it,but they do not live for it. They say, our citizenship "is in heaven; from whence also we look for the coming of the Saviour, the Lord Jesus Christ: Who shall change our vile body, that it may be fashioned like unto his glorious body...whereby he is able even to subdue all things unto himself" (Phil 3:20–21).

We are but strangers and pilgrims in this world; this is a land through which we travel, we are all journeymen. It is true of all of us—here today, gone tomorrow! But if we are in the kingdom of God and have His righteousness, we know that death to us is nothing but to be ushered immediately into the glorious presence of the Lord Jesus Christ, to see Him as He is and to spend our eternity with Him.

So the men and women who are in the kingdom of God and have this righteousness, are those who know that here they must not expect much, but that there they have "an inheritance incorruptible, and undefiled, and that fadeth not away, reserved in heaven" (1 Pet 1:4) by God for all who are citizens of His kingdom, for all who have His righteousness. So whatever may happen to such people in this world they sing as they go along—

In heavenly love abiding,
　　No change my heart shall fear;
And safe is such confiding,
　　For nothing changes here:
The storm may roar without me,
　　My heart may low be laid;
But God is round about me,
　　And can I be dismayed?
　　　　　　　　Anna Laetitia Waring

Of course not!

From Him, who loves me now so well,
　　What power my soul can sever?
Shall life or death? shall earth or hell?
　　No! I am His forever.
　　　　　　　　James Grindlay Small

If you are in the kingdom of God and have His righteousness you will not be afraid of death. You will be afraid of nothing because you know that as a child of God you are destined for heaven, for the place of God, for the everlasting glory. "Seek ye first the kingdom of God and his righteousness" and begin to enjoy the blessings of your Father.

3 NOT WITH OUTWARD SHOW

> And when he was demanded of the Pharisees, when
> the kingdom of God should come, he answered them
> and said, The kingdom of God cometh not with
> observation: Neither shall they say, Lo here! or, Lo
> there! for, behold, the kingdom of God is within you
> (Lk 17:20–21).

THERE ARE THOSE WHO WOULD TRANSLATE that last statement like this: "For, behold, the kingdom of God is among you." We cannot say finally which of the two is right; so it is wise, I believe, to accept both translations.

We are considering together, let me remind you, the basic elements and essentials of the Christian faith. We are doing this because there is so much tragic confusion as to what Christianity really is and it is tragic for this reason. The world is in terrible trouble; all the ideas of men have been tried and have been found wanting. They have been given an opportunity but they have not yielded any results; and men and women at long last are beginning to ask, "Is there any hope, can anything be done?" And it is at that point that the Christian Church appears and she stands before the world and says, "Listen to what we have to say." Here is her message, and I believe that in many senses the world is more ready to listen than it has been for many a long year, but unfortunately, when it does turn to listen, it hears a confused sound.

And as the Apostle Paul says to the Corinthians, "If the trumpet give an uncertain sound, who shall prepare himself to the battle?" (1 Cor 14:8). If the sound is uncertain, then we shall add to the confusion. And that is why nothing is more important than that we should be perfectly clear in our minds as to what this Christian message really is. What does Christianity offer to people; what is it? How can we become Christians? These are the questions which we must answer.

Furthermore, what makes this terrible confusion so utterly inexcusable, of course, is that we have an open Bible before us and we have it in a language that we can understand. If we had no Bible but merely some oral tradition, then there would be some excuse for the confusion. Or if we only had the Bible in a language which we could not understand again there would be considerable excuse. But that is not our position at all, so why is there any confusion? And there is only one answer to that question. It is because men and women, instead of taking the message as it is in the Bible, are imposing their own message upon it. They are approaching it with their philosophies, with their theories, their ideas and their attempts to understand; and they are bypassing what is stated in this Book that is open before them in a language that all can understand.

So my plea is that in all honesty, apart from anything else, we are bound to come back to the Bible. Here are the documents of the early Church; here are the records of how Christianity came into being, of what the Church taught at the beginning and something of what happened as the result of that. Whatever we may make of it, we must at any rate listen to it, and we must say that this is clearly the message of the New Testament. And in particular we must come back to the words and to the teaching and the message of the Lord Jesus Christ Himself.

Now that is what we have been doing. And as a result of turning back we have already seen certain things. We have seen that it is a clear message, that the kingdom of God has drawn near—a message proclaimed by the King Himself. And then He goes on, as we saw, to urge men and women to seek this above everything else, to make it their first priority. "The only hope," He says, "is to be in the kingdom of God."

So the question we now have to face, therefore, is this. What is this kingdom of God that He talks about? Great prominence is given to this theme in the four Gospels—"the kingdom of God" or "the kingdom of heaven". Our Lord was always preaching about it. He put it in different ways but that was His major theme. So we do not have any hope of understanding His message unless we have some clear idea as to what He means when He talks about this. Seek that kingdom first, he said; make sure you are in it and then all these other things shall be added unto you.

So we need to make sure we understand what this kingdom is. There is tremendous confusion about this and it is because these verses from Luke 17 deal specifically with that particular question that we must now consider them together. This is the next step in our approach to this essential message of the Christian faith, and so I would divide up the matter like this. How does the Lord Jesus Christ set up His kingdom? Or, to put it another way, How does the kingdom of God come?

We read in verse 17 that "he was demanded of the Pharisees, when the kingdom of God should come?" That was the question they constantly put to Him, and His reply was: "The kingdom of God cometh not with observation: Neither shall they say, Lo here! or, Lo there! for, behold, the kingdom of God is within you." Here, then is our first point: The way in which this kingdom of God comes is something that has been misunderstood from the very beginning.

We see that here. The Pharisees say to Him in effect, "You are always talking about a kingdom; you say that your coming means that the kingdom of God has drawn near; what is this kingdom of God of yours? How is it going to come and when is it going to come? Isn't it about time," they said, "that you told us?" Then our Lord immediately corrects them, and He corrects them, of course, because He discerns immediately that their whole notion of the coming of the kingdom is entirely wrong.

There is another illustration of exactly this same thing in John 6:30–31. Here the same people came to Him, and "They said therefore unto him, What sign shewest thou then, that we may see, and believe thee? what dost thou work?"—You keep on talking about this kingdom; now we want some sign from you—"Our fathers did eat manna in the desert; as it is written, He gave them bread from heaven to eat." "What are you doing?" they asked; "Moses was God's leader, he was the lawgiver and he gave a sign by giving the manna; what sign are you giving; what evidence are you going to give us that you really are this King that you are talking about and that you are going to bring in a kingdom?"

The Pharisees and Scribes were constantly debating with Him over that very point. You cannot but be struck as you read the four Gospels, and particularly John's Gospel, by how much of their time is taken in mere argument and disputation between our Lord and these Pharisees and Scribes and doctors of the law. What was it about? Well, it was all due to the fact that they were entirely wrong in their notions and ideas about the coming of this kingdom. They would listen to Him and then they would ply Him with their questions. They would say, "When is it coming then? We want some tangible evidence; we are practical men, we are tired of this mere preaching. When will you show us your kingdom?"

But this was not only true of the Pharisees and Scribes, it was equally true of the Roman governor, Pilate. This is what we read in John 18:33–37: here is our Lord standing before Pilate in the judgment hall: "Pilate entered into the judgment hall again, and called Jesus, and said unto him, Art thou the King of the Jews? Jesus answered him, Sayest thou this thing of thyself, or did others tell it thee of me? Pilate answered, Am I a Jew? Thine own nation and the chief priests have delivered thee unto me: what hast thou done? Jesus answered, My kingdom is not of this world: if my kingdom were of this world, then would my servants fight, that I should not be delivered to the Jews: but now is my kingdom not from hence. Pilate therefore said unto him, Art thou a king them? Jesus answered, Thou sayest that I am a king. To this end was I born, and for this cause came I into the world, that I should bear witness unto the truth. Every one that is of the truth heareth my voice."

Pilate, too, you see, was in trouble; he says in effect, "They say you are a king and you say you are a king; what is your kingdom then? I am representing an earthly kingdom, I am the emissary of the Emperor of Rome. I understand a thing like that; but where is your kingdom, if you say that you are a king?" And our Lord's answer is: "My kingdom is not of this world…" It is the answer to the same sort of misunderstanding.

Indeed, and this is still more remarkable, we are told that even His own brothers did not understand it. In John 7:2–7, we read that the time of the feast of tabernacles had arrived: "His brethren therefore said unto him, Depart hence, and go into Judaea, that thy disciples also may see the works that thou doest. For there is no man that doeth any thing in secret, and he himself seeketh to be known openly. If thou do these things, shew thyself to the world. For neither did his brethren believe in him," says John. Our Lord answers his own brothers and He says, "My time is not yet come: but your time is always ready. The world cannot hate you; but me it hateth, because I testify of it, that the works thereof are evil."

That is most significant. His own brothers, born of the same mother, were jeering at Him and mocking Him; "You claim so much for yourself," they said; "if you are what you say you are, then, go up to Jerusalem. Go up to the feast, people will have gone there from everywhere. Stand up before them and make a proclamation, show yourself. What is this you are doing? You claim a lot but you are spending your time here amongst a handful of poor people. What is this? Why don't you do something about it?" They were expecting the kingdom of God to come with some sort of outward show.

But most remarkable of all was the way in which the disciples themselves stumbled over this very thing. Indeed they still stumbled even after His resurrection. We read in Acts 1:4–7, "Being assembled together with them, [our Lord] commanded them that they should not depart from Jerusalem, but wait for the promise of the Father, which, saith he, ye have heard of me. For John truly baptised with water; but ye shall be baptised with the Holy Ghost not many days hence. When they therefore were coming together, they asked of him saying, Lord wilt thou at this time restore again the kingdom to Israel?" Now this is after the resurrection! These men had seen the crucifixion; they had seen Him dead and buried; they had seen that He had risen. They knew that He was the risen Lord, but still they held on to this notion of His restoring again the kingdom to Israel. "And he said unto them, It is not for you to know the times or the seasons, which the Father hath put in his own power."

So even His own chosen apostles are in trouble about this. They say, "Now then, having conquered death and the grave and having risen from the dead, He is surely going to bring in His kingdom now. He taught a lot about it!" And they even venture to ask Him, "Is this the moment when you are going to do it?" So the misunderstanding concerning the kingdom was universal.

Now I have taken you through all that evidence because it seems to me to be most important. You see, the common fallacy in them all is that the kingdom of God is something that comes visibly, externally, that it comes as a result of some momentous action. Their idea was that when the Messiah of God, the great Deliverer arrived, He would be first and foremost a military and a political personage!

These people had been conquered by the Roman Empire; they were disgruntled and unhappy, and they wanted to be set at liberty. They were patriotic Jews who had had a great past and they wanted that great past restored. They had become unimportant, they wanted Israel to be the chief nation in the world, and their idea of the Messiah, the Saviour, was that when He came, He would gather a great army and lead them against the enemy, and then he would rout that enemy. Then, Jerusalem would be the capital city of the universe and He would be the King who should reign over them! That was their notion, so they were expecting our Lord to set up a kingdom.

And that is why we find that extraordinary verse in John 6:15. Our Lord had just worked that tremendous miracle of feeding the five thousand and they were all deeply impressed. Verse 14 runs, "Then those men, when they had seen the miracle that Jesus did, said, This is of a truth that prophet that should come into the world." Then, notice this: "When Jesus therefore perceived that they would come and take him by force, to make him a king, he departed again into a mountain himself alone." He understood their minds; He heard them murmuring to one another, "This man must be the Prophet, we have never seen a miracle like this before. This is that unusual Person whom we have been expecting; this is the Prophet. So then, let's take hold of Him and get Him from here. He should be in Jerusalem, He should be set up as a King!" And they were about to take Him by force to make Him a king in Jerusalem, but He saw it and intercepted it, and He went away from them.

There, then, was the common fallacy with regard to this kingdom of God and unfortunately it is a fallacy that has persisted. I want to be very plain and simple. We are living in a terrible age; it is an age of bombs; indeed it may be the last age of the world. There are many signs and indications of that, and our eternal destiny depends upon our belief or disbelief in this Gospel, so it is important that we should speak plainly. Now the Roman Catholic church has helped this wrong idea of the kingdom to persist when she states that she is the kingdom; for she is political as well as spiritual; the pope is a political personage and nations exchange ambassadors with him. So there it is; this union of church and state, which is found in Rome; and all the persecutions which she carried out arose from this.

But let us be quite honest, even Protestantism has fallen at times into the same error and there have been periods in the history of the world when armies have gathered together to try to compel people to become Christians at the very point of the sword and face to face with death! It is all this misunderstanding about the kingdom.

And, unfortunately, the misunderstanding has persisted even down to our own days. One of the commonest ideas about the kingdom of God in this present century has been that the kingdom comes by reforming the world and by changing it. Now I am old enough to remember the first thirteen years of this present century, and I remember the great age of the so-called "social gospel". That was what people believed. They said, "It used to be thought that you brought in the kingdom of God by preaching; but that was wrong, the Liberal Party will bring it in by passing acts of Parliament." And it was believed that the Liberal Government of 1906 onwards was really legislating the bringing in of the kingdom of God. This is it, they thought; you relieve the poor, you build hospitals, you build better houses, you bring in your welfare state, you bring in your affluent society; and the world is so much better, that you have brought in the kingdom of God! And there are still many who believe that.

Others put it like this. They think that the business of bringing in the kingdom of God is to make protests. Organise your movements and campaigns, and protest against injustices, against bombs and war; and in so doing, and by agitating on social political matters, you are bringing in the kingdom of God! That is their idea of it; Jesus the political social Teacher!

Now this has been the tragedy of the centuries. People complain of the empty chapels and churches today, but why are they empty? I think one of the main reasons is that before the first world war it used to be said that the Tory party was nothing but the Church of England at prayer, and that Nonconformity was nothing but the Liberal Party at prayer; and there was a great deal of truth in it. And so the kingdom of God was regarded as between these two rival parties! The whole thing had been materialised and so men and women began to say, "We do not need our churches or our Bibles any more; the thing has been done! It is happening before our eyes. The kingdom of God has come in a visible manner, we have brought it in by legislation; so what more is there?" And that is why, I believe, the masses are uninterested at the present time.

That, then, is the fallacy with which our Lord deals. That is wrong, He says—"The kingdom of God cometh not with observation." So, then, how does it come? What are the forms of the kingdom of God? Those are the questions that emerge of necessity from what we have been saying. Now there are three main answers to that question, and they are all put before us in the Gospels, in the New Testament teaching.

Firstly, the kingdom of God comes, and came, with the very presence and power manifested by the Lord Jesus Christ Himself. There is a wonderful illustration of that in Luke 11:14–20: "And he was casting out a devil, and it was dumb. And it came to pass, when the devil was gone out, the dumb spake; and the people wondered. But some of them said, He casteth out devils through Beelzebub the chief of the devils. And others, tempting him, sought of him a sign from heaven. But he, knowing their thoughts, said unto them, Every kingdom divided against itself is brought to desolation; and a house divided against a house falleth. If Satan also be divided against himself, how shall his kingdom stand? because ye say that I cast out devils through Beelzebub. And if I by Beelsebub cast out devils, by whom do your sons cast them out? therefore shall they be your judges. But if I with the finger of God cast our devils, no doubt the kingdom of God is come upon you."

Now that is what I mean. The kingdom of God came when the Son of God was in this world. The kingdom of God is a manifestation of the power of God; a manifestation of the fact that God is superior to the elements of nature, that He is superior also to the devils and to everything that is evil. The kingdom of God is God's reign and when Christ was here on earth, and when He worked His miracles and manifested His marvellous powers, He said: "This is the kingdom of God." Not legislation, not one army conquering another, but the manifestation of the power of God. And did you notice what Christ did? He could calm a storm at sea; He could heal the blind, heal the lame, heal the deaf. He could even raise the dead! He was the Master of creation; He was Master over all the devils, and He said that that was proof positive that the kingdom of God had come.

He gave this same answer in a very dramatic manner to poor

John the Baptist. Even John the Baptist went wrong about this. You find that in Matthew 11:1–5: "It came to pass, when Jesus had made an end of commanding his twelve disciples, he departed thence to teach and to preach in their cities. Now when John had heard in the prison the works of Christ, he sent two of his disciples, And said unto him, Art thou he that should come, or do we look for another?" John's trouble was that he had heard that our Lord was preaching, up in Galilee, to some poor people; He was not down in Jerusalem setting Himself up as a king. There He was, surrounded by poor people, and John in the prison in pain and agony sends his two messengers and says, "Look here, I thought you were the Messiah. I said to my disciples, 'Behold, the Lamb of God that taketh away the sin of the world.' Do you know, I am beginning to wonder whether I was right? Are you really the Messiah? Are you really 'he that should come', or are we to wait for somebody else?"

Then we read, "Jesus answered and said unto them, Go and shew John again those things which ye do hear and see: The blind receive their sight, and the lame walk, the lepers are cleansed, and the deaf hear, the dead are raised up, and the poor have the gospel preached to them." He says in effect, "Go back and tell John what you have seen and ask him a question: Can't you see that these are signs of the coming of the kingdom; can't you see the power of God is here? No one has ever done things like this before!" The very miracles worked by our Lord, the manifestations of His almighty power are an indication of the fact that the kingdom of God has come in His person and in His power.

So then, His answer to these Pharisees who ask Him, "When is it going to come?" is "The kingdom of God cometh not with observation." "You are waiting and looking," He says to them, "can't you see that it is among you; can't you see it is happening in your midst; haven't you felt something of the power yourselves? It is here, it is in me and my mighty power which my Father has given me through the Spirit." That is His answer. It has already come in that way.

But, secondly, it comes in another way. Because the kingdom of God is the realm in which God reigns and rules, then the kingdom is present where men and women have subjected themselves to God and to the Lord Jesus Christ, the Son of God. That is the Church, and the Church is a manifestation of the kingdom of God. But let me be perfectly plain and clear about this. When I say "the Church" I am not thinking of an external organisation. That comes into it, but it is not only that. Let me emphasise again that the system known as Roman Catholicism is not the Church, that is not the kingdom of God. That is an earthly state and kingdom with pomp and power. And the kingdom of God has not yet come with pomp and power and show; neither is it in other state churches.

Neither is the Church merely men and women who are church members. For, alas, you can be a member of a church and not be a Christian and, sadly, there are many such. There has been a time in the life of many of us when we were like that; we were members of a church, but we had no idea as to what Christianity was. I was received as a member of a church at the age of fourteen, though I had not the faintest idea as to what Christianity meant. Furthermore I was allowed to take communion, though I had no notion as it its meaning! So I do not mean formal adherence to a society, not just having my name on a church roll; I do not even mean activities within this society.

"So what do you mean?" asks someone. "Do you mean this latest popular idea and stunt that what we need is a 'religionless Christianity?', the teaching of Dietrich Bonhoeffer, that you abolish your churches and cease to have religious rites and ceremonies and worship, and you find the kingdom of God by going out into the world, mixing with people, and there as you mix with them in their needs and troubles, you find the kingdom of God!" One man goes further and says that if you really want to find the kingdom of God, you don't go to churches, you go to the brothels in Algiers and somewhere like that and there you will find it amongst the drink and the prostitution! And he has actually said that in the name of Christianity! But I do not mean that.

So I do not mean a formal institutionalised church nor a

churchless religionless Christianity; but what I do mean is a body of men and women who have believed on the Lord Jesus Christ, and who believe in their hearts that He is the Son of God. I mean a body of men and women who are living to His glory, who know Him and who are here to serve Him. That is what I mean by the Church. He reigns in the hearts of His true believers, in the hearts of those who are constrained by his love. He reigns in those whose chief desire is to know Him and to serve Him and to be aware of His power. That is the Church. It is one of the forms of the kingdom of God and it is its main form at the present time.

When He was in the flesh there it was; He is here now in His people. The Church is the body of Christ and He acts through them; they are "the body of Christ and members in particular" (1 Cor 12:27).

But, according to this teaching, there is to be a third form of this kingdom and that is one which is to come. And, here in Luke 17, He goes on to speak about this to these Pharisees. There is a day coming, he says,—it is "the day of the Son of man" (v 22). It is a day when the kingdom of God will come in a visible, external manner, in a manner when all shall see it and none shall be able to evade it. It has not yet come; this is the third form; this is at the end of the Church Age; this is at the time when Christ comes back again, when He really returns to the earth in a visible bodily form, surrounded by the angels, riding the clouds of heaven. He will come like that, He has said so Himself. "The Son of man," He said, will come "in the clouds of heaven" (Mk 14:62); "every eye shall see him, and they also which pierced him" (Rev 1:7). The kingdom of God will come with great external pomp and glory. He will come in the majesty of His eternal Godhead and He will come to reign, to judge and to set up His everlasting kingdom.

Let me give you His own words in which he said this: "Then answered Peter and said unto him, Behold, we have forsaken all, and followed thee; what shall we have therefore? And Jesus said unto them, Verily I say unto you, That ye which have followed me, in the regeneration when the Son of man shall sit in the throne of his glory, ye also shall sit upon twelve thrones judging the twelve tribes of Israel" (Mt 19:27-28). That is it. The Son of Man will come and sit in the throne of His glory. This is "the regeneration" He says, and this is the great message about the visible form of the kingdom that is to come. It means that when all the elect have been gathered in, the Son of God will return again into this world. He will set up the judgment throne and He will judge the whole world in righteousness. All who do not believe in Him will be consigned to everlasting punishment with the devil and all the evil angels and they will be banished out of His sight.

Then the whole world, the cosmos will be purged of all evil. Nature is now "red in tooth and claw", but it will not be so then—"the wolf also shall dwell with the lamb, and the leopard lie down with the kid; and the calf and the young lion and the fatling together; and a little child shall lead them" (Is 11:6). This is the regeneration, it is coming. Sin and evil will be banished; there will be a realm of glory and He will sit upon His throne in that glory and all who have believed in Him will be with Him; they will reign with Him for ever and for ever. That is coming; it is His own teaching, as it is the teaching of the whole of the New Testament.

So that is the answer to the second question. Those are the three forms which the kingdom of God takes. One of them has already ceased; the other is in operation; the other is yet to come, and that brings me to my third and my last great principle which is this; our relationship to this kingdom.

We have seen that the kingdom is that realm in which He reigns; in which He masters all His enemies; in which He controls all evil and finally disposes of it. And the one thing that matters to His Church is to belong to that kingdom; that is what we should all be concerned about. So the question is, how can I enter this kingdom; how can I be sure that I belong to it? And the answer is that "the kingdom of God," He says, "is within you," or "the kingdom of God is among you."

Now again I must emphasise what this does not mean. It does not mean that I just accept that part of His teaching which agrees with my ideas. You do not enter the kingdom of God like that. There are many people who try to do that. There are those who have got certain ideas about world improvement and reform; they are looking out for the best teaching, they are looking out for the best idea, they want the world to be a better place; they want to be happier themselves. They have read the philosophers; they have read the great religious geniuses; they have read about Confucianism and Buddhism and Hinduism. They have read about the cults and then they come to what they call "the teaching of Jesus" so they read the Sermon on the Mount and they say, "Now there are very good ideas there, we must use them!" And they decide to take this and adapt it in order that they may know something about this kingdom of God! As, for example, Mr Gandhi used to do. He would pick out portions of Christ's teaching and he would adapt them, though he remained a Hindu, and he thought that that was the way of bringing in the kingdom. But it cannot be done like that.

Neither is it done by our trying to imitate Christ. There are many who are trying to do that. We are even being urged to do it by some of these modern representations of Christianity. We are told that His great secret was His selflessness, that He did not consider Himself. He became weak and allowed the world to edge Him out, to do anything they liked with Him They say if you do the same you are in His kingdom; you are imitating Him and you are like Him and that is the way you save yourselves! The imitation of Christ. Becoming selfless, making great acts of self-sacrifice; doing good in the world, trying to improve it and trying to give a helping hand to people. We are told that as we imitate Him, so we introduce ourselves into the kingdom of God! But He gives a lie direct to all such notions.

How do I enter the kingdom? Oh, He says, "the kingdom of God is within you." But how can the kingdom of God be in me; how can it be amongst us? Well, it comes to this—this is His teaching—the kingdom of God is only in me when I recognise who He is. That is the first absolute essential step. I may have admired Him as a great man; I may have admired Him as the greatest political expert that the world has ever known; the one who had the greatest insight, the greatest social reformer. I may have looked at Him in all these ways and admired Him and praised Him; but the kingdom of God is not in me.

The kingdom of God only enters into me when I realise that He is the Son of God incarnate; when I listen to Him saying, "The time is fulfilled, the kingdom of God is at hand." "It is at hand in me," He says in effect, "because I have come from heaven, because I am the Son of God, because I am the one who has come from the glory and have taken on me human nature." By belief in Him as God in the flesh come to redeem me, there I see Him, and the kingdom of God has entered into me. But it does not stop there.

It means that I give a recognition to His demands on me; it means that I say my 'Amen' to the rightness of His teaching. That is what the Pharisees would never do. That is why they were always arguing with Him and giving Him their trick, trap questions and disputing every point with Him. The trouble was that He came and began to expound the law to them. They were the experts in the law; they thought they knew all about it but now He begins to expound it! He starts off His ministry by saying, "Except your righteousness shall exceed the righteousness of the scribes and Pharisees, ye shall in no case enter into the kingdom of heaven" (Mt 5:20).

Now there it is applied, straight and absolute. The Pharisees fasted twice in the week, they gave a tenth of their goods to the poor; "Not good enough," says this Man, "not sufficient!" No that is not enough, it must *exceed* the righteousness of the scribes and Pharisees. What is He talking about? Well, He expounds it; He says, "Verily I say unto you, Till heaven and earth pass, one jot or one tittle shall in no wise pass from the law, till all be fulfilled. Whosoever therefore shall break one of these least commandments, and shall teach men so, he shall be called the least in the kingdom of heaven: but whosoever shall do and teach them, the same shall be called great in the kingdom of heaven" (Mt 5:18-19).

And then He goes on to illustrate what He means. He says,

"Ye have heard that it was said, by them of old time, Thou shalt not kill; and whosoever shall kill shall be in danger of the judgment: But I say unto you, That whosoever is angry with his brother without a cause shall be in danger of the judgment: and whosoever shall say to his brother, Raca, shall be in danger of the council: but whosoever shall say, Thou fool, shall be in danger of hell fire" (Mt 5:21–22).

Then He goes on—"Ye have heard that it was said by them of old time, Thou shalt not commit adultery" (v 27). "Well," says the Pharisee, "I have never committed adultery, I am all right!" "Wait a minute," says Christ: "I say unto you, That whosoever looketh on a woman to lust after her hath committed adultery with her already in his heart." And on He goes. He says, "If thy right eye offend thee, pluck it out, and cast it from thee: for it is profitable for thee that one of thy members should perish, and not that thy whole body should be cast into hell. And if thy right hand offend thee, cut it off, and cast it from thee: for it is profitable for thee that one of thy members should perish and not that thy whole body should be cast into hell" (vs 28– 30).

Then He continues with His teaching about divorce. They just wrote a bill of divorcement and all was well! But He says, "Whosoever shall put away his wife, saving for the cause of fornication, causeth her to commit adultery" (v 32). He goes on, "It hath been said by them of old time, Thou shalt not forswear thyself...But I say unto you, Swear not at all; neither by heaven; for it is God's throne: Nor by the earth; for it is his footstool:...let your communication be, Yea, yea; Nay, nay: for whatsoever is more than these cometh of evil. Ye have heard it hath been said, An eye for an eye, and a tooth for a tooth: But I say unto you, That ye resist not evil: but whosoever shall smite thee on thy right cheek, turn to him the other also. If any man will sue thee at the law, and take away thy coat, let him have thy cloke also" (vs 33–40). And so He goes on with His teaching.

And having the kingdom of God in your heart means that you accept His teaching; that you are not content with your bit of morality; that unlike the Pharisees you say, "He is right; He gives us a spiritual view of them all. He says that God is concerned as much about my motives, as about my deeds; as much about what I think in my heart, as what I actually do with my hands or my feet. God searches the heart and is not content with the mere casual inspection of my superficial actions. It means that I accept His teaching, I cease to argue, I say, That is right, God demands an absolute righteousness of me."

And then it means that I listen to and accept His definition of me. This is the hardest thing of all. What He says about me is that I am lost. "The Son of man," He says, "is come to seek and to save that which was lost" (Lk 19:10)— "They that are whole have no need of the physician but they that are sick. I came not to call the righteous but sinners to repentance" (Mk 2:17). These are the people who are in His kingdom; the people who recognise that they are lost, that they are sick, that they are sinners, that they are hopeless, that they are vile, that they are so bad that they cannot be improved, and that they must be born again.

Have you accepted that? This is how you enter into His kingdom; this is how the kingdom of God comes into you. It comes into you when you see this, when you say, "Yes, it is perfectly true. I have been trying to save myself and I cannot; I have been making my resolutions, I have been trying to be moral and good and I can't do it. I am lost and I am damned. He is right." The moment you say that the kingdom of God has come in you, because you have repented.

And then the next step is, of course, that you submit yourself utterly and absolutely to His way of salvation. You must accept His rule in every respect; you must accept His interpretation of the law and His diagnosis of yourself and now, in your utter helplessness, you must believe and surrender to His way of saving you.

He tells you what it is quite plainly: "The Son of man came not to be ministered unto but to minister and to give his life a ransom for many" (Mt 20:28). "As Moses lifted up the serpent in the wilderness, even so must the Son of man be lifted up:

That whosoever believeth in him should not perish, but have eternal life" (Jn 3:14–15). You must believe that "There is life for a look at the crucified One" and that you can do nothing. You may decide to be good for the rest of your life but it will not save you; you can try to imitate Him, it will damn you all the more. You must come as a helpless, hopeless, sinner and cast yourself at His feet and look into His face.

In other words, we have got to do with Him exactly as one of those ten lepers that were healed did. We read the story in Luke 17:11 and we are told that "one of them, when he saw that he was healed, turned back, and with a loud voice glorified God, And fell down on his face at his feet, giving him thanks." And that is what we must do. We must realise that He brings us into His kingdom by dying for us; by bearing our sins in His own body, by being made the Lamb of God for us; that He bears our punishment and that it is our only way of deliverance and salvation. You believe it and you say:

> Just as I am, without one plea
> But that Thy blood was shed for me,
> And that Thou bid'st me come to Thee,
> O Lamb of God, I come.
>
> Charlotte Elliott

In other words, it means that you make an absolute total surrender, you cast yourself entirely into His hands. You deny yourself, you take up your cross and you follow Him and if you do these things, the kingdom of God is within you. You have entered the kingdom and the kingdom has entered you; because you see that He is everything to you, and you are nothing. You see that Christ is "the Alpha and the Omega", the beginning and the end, "He is the lily of the valley: the bright and morning star. He is the fairest of ten thousand to my soul."

> Thou, O Christ, art all I want;
> More than all in Thee I find.
>
> Charles Wesley

You just give yourself to Him and acknowledge Him as the Son of God and your personal Saviour and your Lord; you say that you require nothing but Him and He is everything to you and you are going to live to His glory. Your one desire is to know Him, to be near Him and to follow Him in order that you may be in that glory with Him in the final regeneration when he comes at the end of time.

4 RIGHTEOUSNESS, PEACE AND JOY

> For the kingdom of God is not meat and drink; but
> righteousness, and peace, and joy in the Holy Ghost
> (Rom 14:17).

WE HAVE BEEN CONSIDERING TOGETHER the fact
that this kingdom of God and the message about it is
entirely different from everything that man knows
by nature; and there is, it seems to me, a wonderful proof of
this. It is that the various views which men and women have of
the kingdom are so different from one another that they cancel
one another out. They contradict one another and that is,
surely, a proof of the fact that they are all wrong.

Now the misunderstandings concerning the kingdom of
God are almost endless in number. In the last chapter, we saw
that some people think of the kingdom of God in a purely
external manner, in a political or social manner. And we saw
how common that misunderstanding of the Gospel is at the
present time. But now we move on to a consideration of exactly
the opposite misunderstanding and this is the view which says
that it is all inside and nothing at all to do with external affairs.
The kingdom of God, according to these people, is "meat and
drink". In other words, they confuse the kingdom of God as it
really is, with religion or with being religious.

Now, as you know, I do not advocate Bonhoeffer's notion
of "Christianity without religion", because I believe it is

wrong, but there is a measure of truth in what he says. The Bible is full of teaching which shows us the difference between the kingdom of God and religion and the practice of religion. In other words, you can be a religious person and still not be a Christian; still not a citizen of the kingdom of God. That is what the Apostle Paul is saying in this verse: "The kingdom of God," he says, "is not meat and drink, it is righteousness, and peace, and joy in the Holy Ghost."

How did he come to say that? Well, the context here is vitally important. Paul was writing this letter to the Christian members of the church at Rome and they were in a muddle. Let nobody think that Christians are perfect; we are not and we do not preach ourselves. We say that we are imperfect, but that we are very much better than we once were, because then we were hopeless! We are not already perfect but we are on the way to perfection. So Christians can be in confusion; they can be in Christ and yet muddled in their thinking. The devil is always there to try to produce the muddle and he had done it in Rome and you notice what they were arguing about. They were arguing about things like this: which day of the week should you observe as the Lord's day? Should it be the first day, or the last? Should you have your sabbath on Saturday or on Sunday? Both sides were convinced that they were right; they were condemning one another and the whole church was divided.

Then there was another question. They had their heathen temples in those days and these people, before they were converted, used to worship in them. They used to eat, there, some of the meat that had been offered to the pagan gods in the temples; but now, having become Christians, some of them thought that it was wrong to do that, while others thought that it did not matter at all. So they were arguing about this also— What should you eat and what should you drink?—and many other questions. And somebody had sent a report of all this disputing to the Apostle Paul.

So he wrote to them and in effect what he said was, "In the name of God what is the matter with you? Do you think the kingdom of God is meat and drink? Is that Christianity? That's not the kingdom of God," he says, "out upon the suggestion! The Son of God did not come from heaven to earth to live and die and rise again simply in order to deal with such questions. No, 'The kingdom of God is not meat and drink', it is something very different. Thank God it is, 'it is righteousness, and peace, and joy in the Holy Ghost'."

Now we are dealing with this because I know that there are many people who are stumbled by this problem. As they see people arguing and wrangling about such things, they say, "If that's Christianity, I am not interested, I do not want it." But I want to show you that all that is an utter, absolute perversion of what the kingdom of God really is. It is not Christianity; Christianity, let me emphasise this again, is not merely a religion, nor is it merely, in the first place, a system of worship.

Let me explain that. Take the Jews who argued so much and wrangled with our Lord and opposed Him. What was the matter with them? They were putting religion before His message and they felt that He was wrong. They did not understand the kingdom of God because they were immersed in their Jewish religion; and it is still the same. Religion can be the greatest enemy of Christianity. There are some people who think that Christianity simply means attendance at a place of worship and nothing more. If they go to a place of worship on Sunday mornings they say, "I am religious!" They have no idea about doctrine, or about truth; they do not even know what they believe, but they go to church on Sunday morning and that is Christianity! But my answer is that that is religion, not Christianity.

Or again, men and women spend their time in arguing about their denominations and they are not interested in anything else. People are interested in their own place of worship, in their own chapel—"my cause" as over against another! They compete and vie and it has been destructive of the true interests of the kingdom of God. That is but religion and nothing else. We must be clear about these things. There are people outside who are offended by that and I do not blame them because that is not Christianity. Now that does not mean that you do not need organisations. You must have them in some shape or form, but if you put your organisation in the top position and say, "This is it!" then you are denying the kingdom of God.

Then there are others who put all their emphasis on particular ceremonies and particular forms. It is quite astounding, but people will argue and quarrel as to the way in which you should pray; whether you should sit or stand or lie on your face on the floor, or what you should do! As if that is the thing that matters in prayer! They do not talk about meeting God, it is the posture that matters! They argue about the Communion Service as to how the man who administers it should dress; whether the wine should be fermented or unfermented. And these become big things that separate people and divide them. That is to turn the kingdom of God into "meat and drink". But, oh, how common it is, and what an offence it is, and rightly so.

So the Apostle gives his negative and blank denial. "If that is your conception of Christianity," he says in effect, "what you do, and the way in which you worship and where you do it, then you are not a Christian at all." That was the trouble, of course, with the woman of Samaria, to whom our Lord spoke one afternoon. She said, "You Jews say that men ought to worship in Jerusalem; we say you should worship in this mountain." And off she went in an argument—here or there, how you do it and so on! But that is not Christianity. Get rid of it once and for all, that is something very different.

Now this really should be self-evident and obvious to everyone. In a sense, we can thank God that we do not have as much of that attitude as we used to. I think the condition of this country is more hopeful today than it was years ago. People then went to church on Sundays out of habit and out of custom. They did not know why they went; they were brought up to do it and they were denominationalists primarily. Thank God that has come to an end. I would sooner see most of such places empty; then we can start afresh and preach the kingdom of God in its purity and in its simplicity.

But let me touch on another aspect of a false view of the kingdom of God, and this is even more important than the last one. I refer to those who confuse Christianity with a kind of morality only. There are so many people who think of Christianity as if it were but a collection of vetoes and prohibitions and restraints. That was the trouble there in Rome. You should not eat this, you should not eat that, and all those other observances. And there they were, experts and punctilios about these particular things. "No," says the Apostle, "Christ did not come from heaven to earth for that reason, that's not Christianity!"

And we can interpret that at the present time in this way. It is to think that you make yourself a Christian by the way in which you live; that if you do not do certain things you are a Christian, but that if you do them, then you are not. So you do not do these things and then, of course, you can criticise others; you can feel that you are better than they are and so you look down upon them. That was the trouble with the Pharisee we read about in Luke 18—"I thank God I am not like other men; I fast twice in the week; I give a tenth of my goods to the poor—how good I am, not like this miserable publican, this sinner fellow!" But that is not the kingdom of God, that is the precise opposite, the thing that the Apostle is here denouncing. But how common this idea is! How many people think of Christianity today as something which is purely negative; something which always makes demands of you, which tells you that if you are going to be a Christian you have got to stop this, that and the other. And it goes no further and never tells you what Christianity gives to you.

So Christianity is confused with morality. It has been very common in this country in all ranks of society. It is what is sometimes called "public school religion", which was started by Dr Thomas Arnold of Rugby. His idea of Christianity was that "it is morality touched with emotion", nothing more! The Christian is the perfect little gentleman, the man who does not do certain things!

But that is not Christianity; that is not the kingdom of God. You can do that yourself. Yet that is what Dr Arnold taught; it was nothing but ethics and morality, a negative, cold, miserable religion, something that was always prohibiting everything and never giving anything at all.

Now it is a part of the preaching of the Gospel to say things like that. I do not defend the Victorians; I think they did great harm to the kingdom of God. They really did bring it down, most of them, to the level of morality and respectability and they made their Sunday a cheerless joyless day. It was not the kingdom of God, it was "meat and drink", and they spent the whole of their time in talking about things like that.

So, according to them, Christianity is that which makes men and women miserable, which makes them feel that they are always failures. They try to be better, and they cannot succeed, but they must go on trying because it is the only way to get into the kingdom of God, to get into heaven. It is by your life and your own activities that you do it; so you go on trying and trying and, in the words of Milton, you "scorn delights and live laborious days", ever trying but never succeeding. It is like the monk in his cell—fasting, sweating, praying; always giving up, always denying, and never receiving anything at all. Meat and drink!

This has been a very very common idea. There has been nothing throughout the running centuries that has so militated against the true idea of the kingdom of God and the glories of the Christian faith and message. That was the system that medievalism, Roman Catholicism in the Middle Ages, clamped upon the church. That was the whole trouble with poor Martin Luther. He wanted to be a good man, he wanted to be a Christian; he did not want to go to hell. He thought he had to do it himself, so he went into his cell and there he was; hopeless! And so many others have tried the same thing, giving up and denying but knowing no joy, no freedom, no peace, no happiness. Striving and sweating but all in vain—"meat and drink"—bothering and arguing and comparing and criticising!

But I thank God that my message is that that is not the kingdom of God! Is it conceivable that the Son of God would ever have left the courts of heaven and humbled Himself and gone through all He went through in life and in death and in the grave and in rising again, if it is only that? The Jews had all that before He ever came. The great moralists and philosophers taught that sort of thing before the incarnation ever took place. That is not Christianity, that is not the message of the New Testament and thank God it is not. The thing is too small. Paul here is sarcastic, he is ridiculing such a view.

What is the kingdom of God to you? Is it church membership; an occasional attendance at God's House, perhaps Easter Sunday morning only or perhaps once or twice in addition? Is the kingdom of God to you doing good; is it not doing this but doing that; being nice and respectable? Is that it? Do you think the Son of God did all He did just for that? Let such a suggestion be ridiculed out of our minds once and for ever! That is not the kingdom of God.

No, "the kingdom of God is not meat and drink; but righteousness..." So the first test always to apply to anything that offers itself to us as the kingdom of God is that of size. If the thing that is offered to you as Christianity is a little thing, it is not Christianity. Christianity is the biggest thing in the universe; it is grand, it is glorious! It is the kingdom of God so it has to be great. It raises big and profound questions; not just little niceties about forms or ceremonies or rituals, or what you do and do not do, and your nice, compact, little life! For the Christian life is never small and neat, it is big, it is vast, and it starts, you see, with this great question of righteousness.

So what is the difference between being punctilious about what I do and do not do, and all these little observances that make me feel so good; what is the difference between that and Christianity? It is that instead of looking at these little matters, and all the minute details of the law, it says, "Wait a minute! Lift up your head, look into the heavens—God! righteousness!" In other words, it tells me to stop thinking about myself in the way that I have been doing, and to look up in the direction of God and of heaven and of my relationship to Him. It is not my morality, not my ideas as to what is right and what is wrong; it is not how I think that men and women should live. No, we are all silenced. "Stop it," says Paul; "God!" The word "righteousness" immediately lifts us into the presence of God, for God is eternally righteous; indeed He *is* righteousness, it is one of the attributes of His holy eternal character, a part of His holiness, a part of His glory. He is essentially right and upright and good and true.

So, it comes and puts a question to me like this: I say I go to church on Sundays; "All right," says the Apostle, "but what I want to know is, what is your relationship to God?" That is righteousness. And so often we find we have never thought about that at all, because what alone mattered was what we were doing, and what we had been brought up to do.

Indeed, there are so many people who call themselves Christians, but who have never really faced the question of how do they stand before God. They have assumed, like the Pharisees, that if you do this, that and the other, you are all right. They have never thought about God; they have never considered their own relationship to Him. But this is what righteousness makes us do. It does not start with us and our behaviour and our ideas and our worships and our rituals and all the paraphernalia. It says, "There is God and there are you; and you have got to meet Him. You will have to stand before Him, face Him, and give an account of your life lived in the body." So we know nothing about righteousness until we have faced that old question of Job's: "How should a man be just with God?' (Job 9:2). You see, we can go through life and never stop to think of that. We live from day to day; we live on our own activities, on our own goodness and we are nice and self-contained and we have never faced this question. "It is appointed unto men once to die, but after this the judgment" (Heb 9:27), and God will judge us in a holy, righteous manner, because "it is He that hast made us and not we ourselves" (Ps 100:3); and He has put certain powers into us and He expects certain things from us.

When the Apostle Paul visited Athens, the theme of his preaching was righteousness. We read about it in Acts 17:16–34. There he was, in Athens, and he saw the place cluttered up with temples, and to his amazement he saw a temple with this inscription on it: "To the Unknown God". "Ah!' said the

Apostle in effect, "here it is. They have got as far as this. They realise that their gods do not explain enough, so there must be a God behind their gods—'the Unknown God'. But they don't know Him." So this was his sermon: "whom, therefore, ye ignorantly worship, him declare I unto you." "He is not," Paul continued, "a God who is worshipped in temples made by hands, because He has given life and being to all things; He cannot be confined to temples. He isn't only in certain buildings, He is everywhere. I want to tell you about this God," he said, "because the matter has become very urgent. In the past He has winked at the times of this ignorance but now He commands all men everywhere to repent. Why? 'Because he hath appointed a day in the which he will judge the whole world in righteousness by that man whom he hath ordained; whereof he hath given assurance unto all men, in that he hath raised him from the dead.' "

The world will be judged in righteousness which means that, having made us in His own image; having endowed us with faculties and powers and propensities sufficient to enable us to live in accordance with His holy law and His way, God will demand that of us. Men and women were made by God to be companions; they were meant to walk with God in a life of obedience to His holy will. There is no sin, no evil, no darkness, no foulness anywhere. It is walking in the light with God as God is light. That is the life of righteousness and every one was meant to walk like that. And the question is, are we walking like that? Because we shall all be judged in those terms and according to that standard.

Nothing matters but this. Our Lord put it like this to the Pharisees. He said: "Ye are they which justify yourselves before men; but God knoweth your hearts: for that which is highly esteemed among men is abomination in the sight of God" (Lk 16:15). That was His indictment of them—that they justified themselves before men. In popular esteem, the Pharisees were very good men; they fasted in the week; they gave a tenth of their goods to feed the poor; they "made broad their phylacteries"; they stood in the market places and showed their wonderful goodness. They were great teachers of the law, in their wrong sense, and people admired them. They said, "What wonderful men!" But look again at our Lord's comment on them: "God knoweth your hearts!"

You see it comes to this. This is the question of righteousness. I have got to stand before God; but look at what I have done; what about my sins, the evil I have committed? It is there and what can I do about it? I must do something, because God knows it all; nothing is hidden from Him; it is in my record, and so I must get rid of it. But not only that, he sees my heart also. He does not only see my deeds, He sees my thoughts, my desires, and my imaginations. He sees the depths of my heart, the very vitals of my being and He is going to judge me according to these things. Man was made perfect; in his heart, his mind and his soul, and he was meant to be perfect in his conduct. That is righteousness. Clean without, clean within, and we have seen that our Lord tells us to seek that as our first priority.[1]

This is what the kingdom of God is about and the moment you realise that, there is not much point in talking about your church attendance, is there? There is not much point in telling me what you eat and what you do not eat; or what you do and do not drink. There is not much point in telling me how much better you are than prostitutes and drunkards; for what does it matter? "God seeth the heart, and that which is highly esteemed among men is abomination in the sight of God."

It was because he had some such conception of righteousness that even Isaiah under the Old Testament dispensation was able to say, "All our righteousnesses are as filthy rags" (Is 64:6). And the same was true of the proud, self-satisfied Saul of Tarsus who thought he was righteous as regards the law, and excelling over all his countrymen in his obeying the commandments of God as he saw it. But it was when he really understood righteousness, that he said, I really now count it all as dung and as loss, "that I may win Christ, And be found in him, not having my own righteousness, which is of the law, but that which is through the faith of Christ, the righteousness which is of God by faith' (Phil 3:9).

Once you understand righteousness as defined by God, all your goodness becomes vile, it becomes manure and refuse; it is ugly, foul and festering; it is putrid. "The kingdom of God is not meat and drink but righteousness."

The question of righteousness is this therefore—"Can the Ethiopian change his skin, or the leopard his spots?" (Jer 13:23). How can I stand before God? What do I do about my past sins? I cannot stand before God unless I am pure and clean, unless I am like God Himself. And the moment you see this, all this fiddling about vestments and the type of wine you use, and a thousand and one of your pettinesses, they are all utterly ridiculous, they have got nothing to do with it!

That is the problem; and here is the answer that a soul gives when it is awakened to that problem:

> Rock of ages, cleft for me,
> Let me hide myself in Thee;
> Let the water and the blood,
> From Thy riven side which flowed,
> Be of sin the double cure,
> Cleanse me from its guilt and power.
>
> Augustus Toplady

I need to be cleansed from guilt and from the power of sin— "Create in me a clean heart, O God; and renew a right spirit within me" (Ps 51:10). That is what I need. I must positively be made righteous. And thank God that is the message of the kingdom of God, that Christ came from heaven to earth and did all He did in order to give me "the double cure"—to cleanse me from the guilt and power of sin. "God," says the Apostle Paul, "hath made him to be sin for us, who knew no sin; that we might be made the righteousness of God in him" (2 Cor 5:21)—"We are ambassadors for Christ," he says earlier, "as though God did beseech you by us: we pray you in Christ's stead, be ye reconciled to God." And what is the ambassador's message? It is this "...that God was in Christ, reconciling the world unto himself, not imputing their trespasses unto them" (2 Cor 5:19–20).

Now to "impute" is to put something in a book, in a ledger, and God, you see, has got your name in His ledger. Oh, yes, it is there. I do not care what your name is; He has an index; your name is there; He opens it at your name and there is the record of everything you have ever committed, is imputed, put to your account in the ledger. It is under your name and you have got to answer for it. But God has taken your account and has put it to His account. That is what imputation means. God made Jesus Christ "to be sin for us." He died to bear my punishment. That is what killed Him. So my guilt has been imputed to Him and it has been taken away from me and therefore I am freely forgiven.

But then there is my other problem, this power of sin, this evil nature. I want a new nature, I want to get rid of the thought of sin and the life and the desire of sin. Before I can spend eternity with God, I must have a clean and a pure heart and a righteous nature. I cannot produce it. What nonsense it is to attempt it! The moment you try you will see your own blackness and darkness; you cannot. You cannot change yourself but, thank God, God can— "...that we might be made the righteousness of God in him."

For when He imputes our sins to Him, He imputes His righteousness to us. This is marvellous! Out of my ledger goes my sin, put to His account; then His goodness, His righteousness, His purity are put into my account under my name! To put it another way, here am I with the black cloak of my sinfulness and I cannot stand, in such a cloak, before God who is light. What God does is to put over my cloak the cloak of the righteousness of Jesus Christ, His perfect spotless life of obedience, His holy nature. I am in Christ, I belong to Him. He is the new man and I am in Him and God sees me in Him clothed with His righteousness—

> Jesus, Thy blood and righteousness
> My beauty are, my glorious dress;
> 'Midst flaming worlds, in these arrayed,
> With joy shall I lift up my head.
> > Nicholaus von Zinzendorf
> > tr. by John Wesley

This is Christianity: not your little goodness and mine; not what I am doing and what I am not doing. Not how much better I am than somebody else; not how much better I am than I once was. No, you forget it all and look to Him. You see His perfect spotless righteousness and you know that if you believe in Him it is given to you and you are clothed with it.

"Peace"—"righteousness and peace". It follows inevitably, does it not? How can people be at peace when they are worried about their souls? How can they have peace when they know they are damned? Or when they are afraid of death because they know that it is followed by judgment? How can men and women have peace when they are striving, only to find how unworthy they are? It is impossible. But the moment they believe this blessed truth of the kingdom of God and in Christ as God's way of righteousness, then everything is changed immediately. "Being justified by faith, we have peace with God." It is an end of all my futile struggles.

Go back to Luther. There it is all in a perfect picture: the striving, and the agony and the restlessness and the pain and all the futility! Then, suddenly he saw it—"The just shall live by faith" and peace came into his soul. What he could never do, Christ had already done for him. And when he saw it peace flooded his soul. As the hymnwriter has put it:

> O happy day that fixed my choice
> > On Thee, my Saviour and my God:
> Well may this glowing heart rejoice,
> > And tell its raptures all abroad.

> 'Tis done, the great transaction's done;
> > I am my Lord's, and He is mine:

> He drew me, and I followed on,
> Charmed to confess the voice divine.
> > Philip Doddridge

Or again,

> Peace, perfect peace, in this dark world of sin?
> The blood of Jesus whispers peace within.
> > Edward Henry Bickersteth

I am no longer filled with a craven fear of God. He is no longer to me some tyrant waiting to pounce on me and to damn me and to hurl me to hell. He is my loving Father who loved me with an everlasting love, with such a love as to send His only Son to die on the Cross for me. And the moment I realise that, I am at peace with Him.

"Having therefore, brethren," says the author of the Epistle to the Hebrews, "boldness to enter into the holiest by the blood of Jesus" (Heb 10:19). For the moment you see that you are made righteous by Christ and clothed in His righteousness, you can go to God with confidence. He is your Father, He is waiting to receive you and you can pray as you have never prayed before. The way is clear, it is a new and a living way that has been opened. You are at peace with God and at peace within; you have found rest for your soul.

As Augustine put it from his own experience—"Thou hast made us for Thyself and our souls are restless until they find their rest in Thee." Thank God for it. Peace with God, peace within and peace with other people, seeing that they are exactly the same as we are and have the same need. We no longer compare ourselves with others, for what is the point of saying that I am better than my neighbour, if we are both damned and lost? Peace with neighbours, because we are together at peace with God.

That is the kingdom of God. Have you found this peace? Is your soul still restless? Are you still struggling with the philosophers and trying to read and understand; are you waiting for a book that is about to appear which you think will help you? Are you proposing to do this or that? Oh, the restlessness and the futility of it all! Stop, it will never bring you anywhere. Say to Him, before you go any further,

> Not the labours of my hands
> Can fulfil Thy law's demands;
> Could my zeal no respite know,
> Could my tears for ever flow;
> All for sin could not atone;
> Thou must save, and Thou alone.
>   Augustus Toplady

Tell Him that and you will find rest for your troubled soul. And Paul's last word follows of necessity—"Joy in the Holy Ghost." A Christianity which does not make you happy is not worthy of the name. But as long as you are just moral you will never be happy; you will never know the joy of the Holy Ghost. But the kingdom of God, the faith of the New Testament, is vibrant with joy. Look at the people on the day of Pentecost, who were baptised with the Holy Spirit. They were so happy that people thought they were drunk! They said, "These men are full of new wine" (Acts 2:13). Why? Because they were elated, exalting and triumphant; they were glorying in Him. That is Christianity.

The exhortation of the Apostle Paul to the Philippians is, "Rejoice in the Lord alway: and again I say, rejoice" (Phil 4:4). If you are not rejoicing, you are not a Christian. Not the joy that the world gives because that is no good. It comes and goes, it is fitful, changing with my changing mood. If I hear a threat of war then it has gone and we are all in a panic. No, the joy of the Holy Ghost is the joy of men and women who know their sins are forgiven, the joy of someone who, as John Bunyan pictures it in *Pilgrim's Progress* has been carrying that terrible load of sin, and then suddenly sees it tumbling down the road; the Cross has got rid of it.

These things do not need to be argued over. If you know

your sins are forgiven you must be a very happy person and conversely if you are not happy it is because you do not know that. If you are still trying to make yourself a Christian you have not got the joy of the Holy Ghost, and never will have. Christianity as something to be attempted by man is of all things the most impossible—the Sermon on the Mount is there at the very beginning to tell us how impossible it is. Go out and imitate Christ, if you like to talk about such things; but you will be the most miserable wretch on earth. The imitation of Christ has never given happiness, never! It is of all things the most depressing. Monasticism was depressing, the Jews' religion was the same and a false Christianity is depressing, since it produces miserable people. All they know is that they must not do this and that so they try not to and try to be better, yet they are miserable and always worrying about themselves and their little souls and their sins. Misery, wretchedness, is the antithesis of the kingdom of God.

But not only are my sins forgiven, I know that I am in this new relationship. I am not only forgiven, I have become a child of God, even as I am; He has adopted me into His family. And if you do not feel that you are happy because of that, then you do not know anything about Christianity. When some great honour comes to you you are full of rejoicing, and you tell everybody, do you not? So then, if you have really believed that in Christ you are in the family of God, you must tell the whole world about it and you must be filled with rejoicing. You are a child of God, you have His Spirit in you—"joy in the Holy Ghost."

And perhaps one of the most wonderful characteristics of this joy is this fact that it is something which makes one entirely independent of circumstances. The trouble with the worldly joy, as we have said, is that it comes and goes. It varies with the wind, depending entirely upon international conditions and many another thing, whereas the joy of the Holy Ghost is independent of everybody and everything.

"Not only that," says Paul, "but we glory in tribulations

also" (Rom 5:3). Even though everything is against us, we still rejoice, because our joy does not depend upon what is happening to us, but upon the great facts that we have just been considering. Throw us into prison, He is with us; He has said: "I will never leave thee, nor forsake thee" (Heb 13:5), and He does not.

That is why His people, His saints and martyrs and confessors have been able to sing even on the scaffolds. They sang as they were thrown to the lions in the arena; they sang as they were burnt at the stake at the time of the Protestant Reformation. They have done it ever since, and they go on doing it.

Take those magnificent words that were written by the Apostle Paul when he was actually in prison. This is the sort of thing that the Christian can say and testify because he has the joy of the Holy Ghost: "Not that I speak in respect of want: for I have learned, in whatsoever state I am, therewith to be content. I know both how to be abased, and I know how to abound; everywhere and in all things I am instructed both to be full and to be hungry, both to abound and to suffer need. I can do all things through Christ which strengtheneth me" (Phil 4:11–13). That is the joy of the Holy Ghost! It does not matter where you are; if you cannot attend a place of worship, you still have it and nobody can rob you of it. They can cut your tongue off but they cannot take your joy from you. They can blind you but still you see Him with the eye of faith. "A joy unspeakable and full of glory" (1 Pet 1:8).

And finally what makes it so wonderful is that it is "the hope of glory" (Col 1:27). "To me to live is Christ," says Paul, "and to die is gain"; for it means "to be with Christ which is far better" (Phil 1:21,23). This joy cannot be quenched, it cannot be removed, it cannot be destroyed. It does not matter what people may do to you; they can even kill you, but when they do, they simply usher you immediately into the presence, into the glory, unto Him who loved you and whom you now love in turn. It is the joy of the Holy Ghost.

That and that alone is Christianity. This is the kingdom of

THE KINGDOM OF GOD

God, not meat and drink but righteousness and peace and joy in the Holy Ghost.

---

[1] Chapter 2.

5 THE MYSTERY

The disciples came, and said unto him, Why speakest
thou unto them in parables? He answered and said
unto them, Because it is given unto you to know the
mysteries of the kingdom of heaven, but to them it is
not given. For whosoever hath, to him shall be given,
and he shall have more abundance: but whosoever
hath not, from him shall be taken away even that he
hath. Therefore speak I to them in parables: because
they seeing see not; and hearing they hear not, neither
do they understand. And in them is fulfilled the
prophecy of Esaias, which saith, By hearing ye shall
hear, and shall not understand; and seeing ye shall see,
and shall not perceive: For this people's heart is
waxed gross, and their ears are dull of hearing, and
their eyes they have closed; lest at any time they
should see with their eyes, and hear with their ears,
and should understand with their heart, and should be
converted, and I should heal them. But blessed are
your eyes, for they see: and your ears, for they hear.
For verily I say unto you, That many prophets and
righteous men have desired to see those things which
ye see, and have not seen them; and to hear those
things which ye hear, and have not heard them (Mt
13:10–17).

IN THIS PASSAGE, which follows the parable of the sower, we come to yet another misunderstanding of the kingdom of God, and this is a particularly important one, because it deals with the whole question of how we approach it, how we listen to it. You notice our Lord's word here at the end of His parable: "Who has ears to hear, let him hear." But not only that, the very parable itself directs our attention to this, especially the question that was put by the disciples and the answer that our Lord gave to them. The disciples, you see, were surprised that our Lord spoke to the people in parables. This is a curious thing to do, they said; "why speakest thou unto them in parables?" According to Mark's Gospel, they did not put the question to Him until a little later, when they had gone into the house and when they were alone; and it was then that our Lord gave the answer to their question.

This is an important question for us to consider because it throws great light and, indeed, gives the final answer to what, I would say, is the chief misunderstanding of the message concerning the kingdom of God. What people are really saying can be put like this: "You know, there is really only one big obstacle to people becoming Christian and that is these outmoded ways of thinking, this out-moded terminology that you have in the Bible. What we have got to remember," they continue, "is that we do, after all, happen to be living in the twentieth century. Modern men and women are secular and scientific, and because of the advance of knowledge, the benefit of which they are reaping, they are offended by these old modes of thought, this idea of the miraculous and the supernatural! They can't take it; they know it is not true because science has proved it is not! As long as you go on giving your Gospel to them mixed up with all these things, then, of course, you can't expect them to listen! And," they conclude, "why should they listen? Let's give it to them in the right way; let's drop all this. It may have been all right four hundred years ago, or still more two thousand years ago, but not now!"

Now that is surely one of the commonest attitudes to the preaching and to the hearing of the Gospel. That is the problem.

"He who hath ears to hear, let him hear." But how do you hear; how do you listen; what can we do in order to enable people to do so?

In order, therefore, to put this position quite clearly, these people often say something like this. They say, "What is needed, of course, is the simple message of the Gospel. Look at the way our Lord spoke—in parables. Why did He do this? Well, he did so," they say, "in order to make it plain and clear. He told them a story, you see. He didn't put it in such great terms as justification and sanctification! No, of course not! The glory of the Master"—as they call Him—"was that He was always so simple. He took a simple illustration; He said, 'It is like this', and, of course, everybody understood!"

"Now," they continue, "we have got to come back to that. Let us have none of your theology; none of this old terminology; none of these out-dated ideas that the Reformers in the sixteenth century may have liked, but which we now, of course, because of our greater knowledge, cannot possibly accept! We must use a language that everybody can follow and then they will see it, they will believe it and they will go out and put it into practice! That's the way to save the Christian Church, that's the way to make men and women Christian!"

And what is truly incredible is that the words spoken by our Lord in this passage seem to have been uttered specially and specifically to answer, to refute, and to denounce completely this modern idea, so that is why I am calling your attention to it.

I do not do so because I want to be controversial. I wish that all God's people spoke the message as it is before us. But we are driven to this because unless this message is believed as it is, there is no salvation in it; and as our eternal destiny depends upon our being right about this, then we must consider it. There is no hope unless we are in the kingdom of God. But what is it and how can we enter it? What is more important than that? When there are false guides about, it is essential that those who adhere to the simple statements of the Gospel should be heard.

So let me try to show you how, in this very passage, even if we had nothing else, our Lord shows us once and for ever how completely wrong all that other view is. I will put it to you in the form of a number of propositions.

Firstly, the Christian message and way of life is a mystery— "Why speakest thou unto them in parables? He answered and said unto them, Because it is given unto you to know the mysteries of the kingdom of God." Now this is the first basic foundational principle. If we are wrong at this point, of course, we will be wrong everywhere else.

The whole of this modern idea is based on the notion that this Christian truth is something which is manifest and simple, and that if we can only get rid of all this accumulation of false thinking and that old terminology, then men and women will see this delightfully clear message, the plain teaching of Jesus, and will immediately believe it and act upon it! "The whole trouble," people say, "is due to this lack of clarity of expression—all this about miracles and so on! That is the hindrance." But all that is based upon the assumption that men and women, as they are by nature, are capable of understanding it; capable of following it; and able to put it into practice.

Indeed, as I read this passage, I see at once that all this is not only wrong but dangerously, tragically wrong. "I speak in parables," our Lord says, "because the kingdom of God is a mystery," which is the exact opposite of what we are being told. His whole case, as I want to show you, is that it is *not* clear, but that it is, indeed, very surprising. What He says about it everywhere is that it is totally and completely unlike anything that the natural man has ever heard of or can ever imagine. Furthermore, He goes so far as to say that no man can possibly believe this and begin to understand it until he has been "born again", until he has a "new mind", until he is "born of the Spirit" and has an entirely new understanding. And the word which He uses to express all that is this word "mystery". The message of Jesus Christ concerning the kingdom of God is neither obvious nor simple. It is not a plain message, something that anyone as they are can understand and say, "Oh, how wonderful, how delightful!", and then accept it and practise it. It is a mystery, and the New Testament records prove that.

To start with, we are constantly told even about our Lord's own disciples that they misunderstood, they could not follow Him. They were amazed at what He said and the way in which He said it and they asked Him questions. If you read the four Gospels, you will find that happening constantly, especially when He came to talk about His death and resurrection. When He said that He was going to die, Peter said, "Be it far from thee Lord, this shall not be unto thee" (Mt 16:22). And our Lord had to rebuke him, saying, "Get thee behind me, Satan... for thou savourest not the things that be of God, but those that be of men" (Mt 16:23). The disciples were confused and bewildered, so that when he died they were completely downcast and crestfallen. They did not know where they were nor what to do, in spite of all His teaching.

So it does not seem to have been quite as plain and simple as we are being told, does it? Here were the men who had been with Him day after day after day for three years, and yet even they were in trouble and could not follow it. Or again, Nicodemus, the leader and teacher in Israel, also, as we shall see, found difficulty in understanding this. And Christ's response to him was: "The wind bloweth where it listeth, and thou hearest the sound thereof, but canst not tell whence it cometh, and whither it goeth: so is every one that is born of the Spirit." "Marvel not that I said unto thee, Ye must be born again" (Jn 3:8,7). It is different, it is a mystery; do not try to understand.

And when you consider the Pharisees and Scribes and Sadducees who argued so much with our Lord you find the trouble with them also was that they had not begun to understand it. They thought they did but they had not. Their questions were stupid, even ridiculous; they were thinking in different categories, and never really made contact with our Lord, because what He was talking about is a mystery. It is unlike man's natural ideas or religion, it is unlike man's philosophy. It is altogether different; it is unique.

The Apostle Paul wrote exactly the same thing to the Corinthians. He says, "Howbeit we speak wisdom among them that are perfect: yet not the wisdom of this world, nor of the princes of this world, that come to nought: But we speak the wisdom of God in a mystery, even the hidden wisdom which God ordained before the world unto our glory." He continues, "The natural man receiveth not the things of the Spirit of God: for they are foolishness unto him: neither can he know them, because they are spiritually discerned" (1 Cor 2:6–7,14). That is a very strong statement, and Paul makes similar statements in other places. In 1 Corinthians 4:1 he says that he and the other Apostles are "stewards of the mysteries of God" and in 1 Timothy 3:9 he refers to "holding the mystery of the faith in a pure conscience."

Now a mystery in the New Testament is a truth that is hidden from the natural man, it is something that he has to be shown. The term was used with regard to the "mystery religions" that were common and popular in that ancient world, and it is a term that is used today. I believe that there is a certain secret society to which people belong. They have to go through a process of what is called "initiation" to enter it, and it is there that they are let into the secret, and the mystery is divulged to them. It is exactly the meaning that is used here in the New Testament with regard to the message concerning the kingdom of God. The very term tells us that in and of ourselves, and by our natural abilities, we cannot understand or follow it. It must be revealed to us.

As our Lord puts it in this passage in Matthew 13, "...it is given unto you to know." In other words, it is given to you to know but it is not given to the others. Now that is a perfect account of a mystery. You can try your best to arrive at it and to understand it but you cannot, it is something that must be revealed; a veil must be drawn back and suddenly you are shown it.

Our Lord continues, in verse 12, "For whosoever hath, to him shall be given, and he shall have more abundance: but whosoever hath not, from him shall be taken away even that he hath. Therefore speak I to them in parables: because they seeing see not; and hearing they hear not, neither do they understand."

Now is that clear? Why did our Lord speak in parables? Was it like a man using illustrations today or telling stories in order that the thing might be made simple and clear so that everybody can follow it? It was the exact opposite. He spoke in parables because had He spoken directly, had He told them exactly who he was, why he had come, and the consequences of that, then He would have been killed at the very outset of His ministry.

He knew that, so He deliberately spoke in parables, so that, at one and the same time, the meaning could be made clear to His followers, but concealed from the others. That is what He said Himself; He spoke in parables knowing that they would not understand Him. The men who finally did kill Him hated Him the moment He began to speak plainly, and they said, "Away with Him, crucify Him." But here in this passage that time had not yet come, so He gave His teaching. He wanted to build up His own people, to leave this message behind Him in the world, so He spoke in parables. It was plain to the ones it was meant for, but not to the others, who heard words but did not understand; they saw but did not perceive.

There is only one conclusion to draw from all this. The message concerning the kingdom of God is not something that is obvious to the natural man, it is in itself a mystery and it is a mystery to all men by nature.

That, then, is our first principle, and the second is this. What is the greatest hindrance to the understanding of this mystery? According to that other view all we need is new terminology. There was a time when people thought that if only we had the Bible in modern English then everyone would believe it. Now they are suggesting that we leave out most of it, and just have this simple ethical moral teaching left for those who are anxious for such things.

But, is *that* the hindrance? Is it merely a question of up- to-date language, or just that we must be scientific in our ideas and terminology? Has the passage of the centuries made any difference? Listen to our Lord. "Those," He says in effect, "are not the hindrances." What, then, are they?

The first and foremost hindrance to an understanding of this message concerning the kingdom of God is nothing but pride of intellect—"they seeing see not; and hearing hear not, neither do they understand" (v 13). That was the whole trouble with these Pharisees and Scribes and doctors of the law. They were the men who knew! They said, "We see, we know, we hear, we understand!" That is why they got nothing from Him and that is why they eventually crucified Him. And that is why people are not Christian; that is why they have always not been Christian. It is confidence in their own knowledge, in their own ability. There is no difference at all; it was like that when Christ was here, it has been like that ever since.

Our Lord once put it like this. He turned to His Father in heaven and said, "I thank thee, O Father, Lord of heaven and earth, because thou hast hid these things from the wise and prudent, and hast revealed them unto babes. Even so, Father: for so it seemed good in thy sight" (Mt 11:25–26). The common people "heard Him gladly", it was the know-alls, the Pharisees, the proud intellects, the people who thought they had got life taped and understood everything, it was they who rejected Him. And the Apostle Paul repeats this when he says, "Ye see your calling, brethren, how that not many wise men after the flesh, not many mighty, not many noble, are called" (1 Cor 1:26). Why not? So that "no flesh should glory in his presence", but rather "he that glorieth, let him glory in the Lord" (1 Cor 1:29,31).

There is no greater obstacle to a belief in this message, to an understanding of the kingdom of God, than this pride of intellect. Modern men and women say, "Am I to believe what they believed four hundred years ago? Out upon the suggestion! Look at how I have advanced since. Am I to believe what people believed in the first century?" They say, "This is insulting! Can't you see the march of time, the advance of intellect. Have I got to go back, must I be born again? Are you saying that I am a fool, that all my knowledge is of no value?" But that is precisely what I am saying. That is what our Lord said.

But that is not the only hindrance. Another one is, of course, prejudice—"their eyes they have closed; lest at any time they should see with their eyes, and hear with their ears, and should understand with their heart, and should be converted, and I should heal them" (v 15). "That's why people don't understand," says our Lord in effect. "It isn't terminology, it is prejudice; they have deliberately shut their eyes." They have decided not to look or listen; they have dismissed Christianity without ever having heard it.

And this is still the commonest cause of dismissing it. People say, "There is nothing in Christianity; it's played out, ridiculous!" And then you say to them, "But what about this or that?" And they have never heard of it. So they really do not know the case for Christianity and the thing is very pathetic indeed. If you listen to their discussions on the television and radio you will see it coming out endlessly. Read their articles and their books. It is really childish. They have never read the Bible, they have never faced the case, they have shut their eyes deliberately. They say, "Not at all, I am not going to give in to that." They do not want to hear it, they do not want to be disturbed; they are settled that they know what is right, that they can put themselves right and live as they think they should live. Prejudice!

These are the causes why men do not understand the mystery. The Pharisees never listened to our Lord. They said, "This man is against us, He's never been trained as a Pharisee. This carpenter! This man must be put down." So they twisted everything He said. Even when he healed a man, they would find fault with Him. Nothing He did was right. That is sheer prejudice. And you, have you ever given this a fair hearing; have you really looked at this message; have you ever come with an open mind? Of course you have not! We are born with prejudices. We think it is clever to deny Christianity. That is sheer prejudice.

But there is a third cause, and this is how our Lord puts it:

"This people's heart is waxed gross, and their ears are dull of hearing" (v 15). I rather like John Wycliffe's translation of this phrase. He wrote, "Their heart is enfattened." That is a very good description. It is a picture of a heart that has got so much fat round it that it cannot work properly. If you know any medicine you will be aware that there is such a thing as a "fatty heart". There can be so much fat in your heart that your muscles cannot work properly and it will kill you. That is what is the matter with these people spiritually, says Isaiah, and our Lord quotes him in agreement. They are so fat that they are dull and stupid. Their heart is "waxed gross"; they have got fatty degeneration of their minds, of their morals and of their spirits. They have been so over eating and over drinking and so over indulging their sense that their minds cannot function. That is what it really means. He is describing carnality.

There is a man in the Old Testament called Esau and in the New Testament he is described as "a profane person" (Heb 12:16). A profane person is a man who has given himself exclusively to the things of this world, who is interested in eating and drinking, indulging his powers and so on; a secular man. He is taken over by what our Lord, in His exposition of the parable in this passage, calls "the cares of this world, and the deceitfulness of riches" (v 22).

That is why people are not Christian, they eat too much, they drink too much, they look too much at their television. They are filled with their worldliness, with everything that discourages thought about the soul and about God and about heaven and hell and eternity. They are so "enfattened" and dulled and stupid and paralysed by it all that if you talk to them about God and the mystery of His kingdom, they do not know what you are talking about, they are unable to follow it. All their faculties have become atrophied, they cannot listen to long sermons, everything must be short and brief. It must be looked at and be exciting, everything must be in a kind of potted form. Their hearts are enfattened, their minds and their morals are suffering from obesity and so they cannot really think and reason as they should.

There, then, according to our Lord, are the main hindrances to an understanding of the mystery of the kingdom of God. Of course, we do not like that, do we? It is much nicer to say, "I am a scientific person, you know, and I do not believe in this three- storied universe. I do not believe in things like that—hell down below, earth, and heaven. No, being scientific, I must have it up-to-date. Drop the miraculous and then I am prepared to listen." Now I sometimes feel that I am too old to listen to that sort of nonsense; the New Testament certainly is much too old to listen to it! The Pharisees put up a wonderful camouflage but our Lord penetrated it. He said, "Your trouble is your pride, your prejudice and your enfattened mind and reason."

So we have seen the fact that the Christian message is a mystery. Secondly we have considered the greatest hindrances to the understanding of this mystery and now my third proposition is the content of the mystery. What is it? Oh, it is the good news about God healing: "This people's heart is waxed gross, and their ears are dull of hearing, and their eyes they have closed; lest at any time they should see with their eyes, and hear with their ears, and should understand with their heart, and should be converted, *and I should heal them*" (v 15). That is the message; the marvel of God's way of salvation. The mystery is that God before the very foundation of the world had planned and purposed it all. That is what Paul means when he talks about "the hidden wisdom"—"We speak," he says, "the wisdom of God in a mystery, even the hidden wisdom, which God ordained before the world unto our glory" (1 Cor 2:7). This is what the world knows nothing about.

For the message of the Bible from beginning to end is about nothing but God's plan of salvation, God's great purpose of redemption. It is a mystery the man of the world is not interested in and knows nothing about. But that is the message of the kingdom. In the Old Testament you see not so much the history of the Jews, as the history of God bringing into purpose and into action this great plan and purpose of His. God made the whole world; He made all men and women, but we all sinned against Him, and what God did was this. He just took a man and turned him into a nation. This is the mystery of God's action. He did not deal with the whole world in the Old Testament but just with this one nation. He gave it messages, He gave it leaders, and He gave it revelation. He let them partly into the secret, while the rest of the nations were in absolute ignorance, living the life of pagans, worshipping other gods in utter darkness. Israel alone had got it. That is the mystery of God's kingdom and of God's way.

But it is God's plan ultimately to deal with the whole world—in the Old Testament it is Israel only but that is preparatory—His purpose is to bring in all nations. Thus the Apostle Paul in writing to the Ephesians, is able to say, "How that by revelation he made known unto me the mystery; (as I wrote afore in few words)... Which in other ages was not made known unto the sons of men, as it is now revealed unto his holy apostles and prophets by the Spirit; That the Gentiles should be fellow- heirs, and of the same body, and partakers of his promise in Christ by the gospel" (Eph 3:3,5–6). Some of the Old Testament prophets had glimpses of it, but they did not understand it clearly. It was a mystery hidden even from them; intimations were given though not the full thing; but here is God's plan unfolding. God will head up everything again in Christ. That is His great and glorious purpose which the world knows nothing about.

But the mystery began to become more evident at this crucial point when the Son of God came into this world. Take verse 17 in our passage: "For verily I say unto you, That many prophets and righteous men have desired to see those things which ye see, and have not seen them; and to hear those things which ye hear, and have not heard them." "Look," says Christ in effect, "I am the mystery. Look at me, this is the kingdom of God, I am the King, I am the bringer-in of the kingdom. Do you know," He says, "in centuries past men longed to have a glimpse of this; they longed to hear the words that I am speaking to you; but they died and never saw it; they only saw it afar off. They longed to know, but you are having the actual privilege; the mystery is being unfolded before you; I am the mystery!" Christ Himself!

Here is the mystery of the kingdom of God. Its message is not some ethical teaching as to what I am to do or not to do. It is not how I stop war or this or that; nor is it some practical message that I can put on statute books. No, this is what Paul says, "And without controversy great is the mystery of godliness: God was manifest in the flesh, justified in the Spirit, seen of angels, preached unto the Gentiles, believed on in the world, received up into glory" (1 Tim 3:16). What a mystery it is—His own blessed Person!

Now men and women had expected Him to come as some great royal prince or personage; they expected Him to be born in a palace, with His arrival heralded by an unusual phenomenon, some great announcement for the whole universe. And, if I may venture to use such language, He slipped in, unobserved and unheralded to the masses, in a stable in a little place called Bethlehem, and His little body was put in a manger. Here is the mystery, the mystery of love, the mystery of the incarnation.

We sing about these things at Christmas-time and it seems to me sometimes that we confine it far too much to that time of the year. Consider this hymn:

> Christians, awake! salute the happy morn,
> Whereon the Saviour of mankind was born;
> Rise to adore the mystery of love
> Which hosts of angels chanted from above:
> With them the joyful tidings first begun
> Of God Incarnate, and the Virgin's Son.
>
> John Byrom

That is the mystery of the kingdom. It is so unlike everything that man has ever thought or imagined. Who would have thought that the Son of God would be born of a Virgin, with not even a human father, and born in such abject poverty and in such hopeless conditions. But look at Him, who is He? God and Man, two natures in one Person.

But let us consider the greatest mystery of all: how does He save? He came into the world to save us, to heal us, to give us deliverance from all our captivity and to give us health. Did He do it by just teaching us; by just giving us a moral ethical example; or by just standing before us and saying, Rise up and imitate me and follow me? Thank God He did not, for if He did we would all be damned and lost.

No, He did it in a manner that the world ridicules, He did it by dying upon a Cross. "We preach Christ crucified," says Paul, "unto the Jews a stumblingblock, and unto the Greeks foolishness." But it is God's way. Christ is "the power of God and the wisdom of God" (1 Cor 1:23–24). He saved by dying, by being "numbered with the transgressors" (Is 53:12), by dying in utter abject weakness. His body was taken down and buried in a grave and it seemed to be the end of Him. And the world laughs at this. What is the point of talking about simple language, new terminology and modern ideas? No, this is eternity. This happened, in time, once and for ever. Men and women have never understood it; they still do not understand it, and they never will by nature. It is a mystery, but it is God's way of salvation.

But it goes on. There, on the Cross, He made the way of healing, but how does it come to me? Now our Lord spoke the parable of the Sower to teach that. He said it is like a man sowing seed. You do not come into the kingdom in mass movements; nor do you come in in families. No, "strait is the gate, narrow is the way" (Mt 7:14). Everyone on their own, everyone must be born again. This does not happen at the point of the sword, compelling people, nor by Acts of Parliament— certainly not! It is by preaching; the seed of the Word and the Holy Spirit applying it.

This is a great mystery; it happens down in the depths of the soul. You are not aware of anything happening for a while, but then it begins to happen. Those close to you do not know that something is happening in you. You look the same, nobody can tell there is any difference, but the operation of God has been going on like a seed in the earth and there is some new life coming in. It is the mystery of salvation, regeneration, rebirth and all the activity of the Spirit.

Not only that, there are blessings which are given to all who receive this message and are born again—"Whosoever hath, to him shall be given, and he shall have more abundance" (Mt 13:12), and we have considered some of these things together: forgiveness, adoption, daily blessings, His abiding presence—more abundance!

But finally, consider the future glory that is awaiting us. This is the mystery of the kingdom. In this world we shall have tribulations. People will persist in thinking of the Christian message as one that is going to reform the world and put it right and we are all going to live happily ever after! But that is a direct contradiction of the biblical message, which states, "In the world ye shall have tribulation" (Jn 16:33). And we have had them and we shall continue to have them. This old world will never be put right—it is doomed and damned.

But here is the mystery. When Christ comes back again He will get rid of all this; He will purge this old universe of evil and He will set up His own kingdom of glory. There will be "new heavens and a new earth, wherein dwelleth righteousness" (2 Pet 3:13), and those who believe in Him shall be in it—"more abundance".

> 'Tis mystery all! The immortal dies!
> Who can explore His strange design?
> In vain the first-born seraph tries
> To sound the depths of love divine
> 'Tis mercy all! let earth adore,
> Let angel minds inquire no more.

So writes Charles Wesley. Or again, he writes,

> Stronger His love than death or hell,
> Its riches are unsearchable;

The first-born sons of light
Desire in vain its depth to see;
They cannot reach the mystery,
The length, and breadth, and height.

God only knows the love of God;
Oh that it now were shed abroad
In this poor stony heart!

That is the language of the man who has seen it. It is God alone who knows it. Not even the angels in heaven can understand it. It is the mystery of God's eternal love.

Therefore, my last principle is this. Had you realised that, in the light of all this, even considering this mystery becomes a judgment to you? "Because it is given unto you to know the mysteries of the kingdom of heaven, but to them it is not given. For whosoever hath, to him shall be given, and he shall have more abundance: but whosoever hath not, from him shall be taken away even that he hath."

It is a very serious and solemn thing to consider the teaching concerning this mystery. It divides the whole of mankind into two groups—and there are no others. "Unto him that hath shall be given." Such a person has a ready mind, a readiness to listen and to learn; he has this good soil, this good earth that is ready to receive and that can respond. He has it and if he has he will receive more and more abundance.

But what of the man who "hath not"? Did you notice this extraordinary phrase: "but whosoever hath not, from him shall be taken away even that he hath." This is expressed more clearly in Luke's corresponding passage where he puts it like this: "But unto whosoever hath not, from him shall be taken even that which he seemeth to have" (Lk 8:18). That, you see, is your wise man, your man of knowledge, your twentieth-century post-war secular man, your atomic worldly man, the man of the space age; this great modern man who looks back in disdain upon the previous centuries because of his advance! Do not ask him to believe what men believed at the time of the Reformation, the thing is monstrous in the light of all our advances! He has so much insight, understanding and learning; he is well equipped; he has got it, and because he has so much, he does not receive the Gospel! But listening to this Gospel becomes a terrible condemnation to him. He refuses it because he thinks he has got so much, but he will find one day that he has nothing.

It simply means that all our modern knowledge and scientific interest do not tell us anything about the vital questions. All the advances in knowledge have not added anything to my knowledge of man himself. They have not told me anything new about the soul; they have not shown me at all how to live, how to avoid sin, how to be pure and moral and clean. They fail to help you how to live when things go wrong, and you have nothing to fall back on. When your loved one dies, how does your science help you? When you are on your own death bed, where does your scientific knowledge come in? And how will it help you on the Day of Judgment when you stand before God and have to give an account of yourself as a living soul, as one who was created in the image of God and who had an opportunity of hearing the message concerning the kingdom? Tell me—where will it be then?

Or of what value will it be to you to say, "I have lived a good life, I have done a lot of good"? Our Lord has already answered you. He says, "Ye are they that justify yourselves before men" (Lk 16:15). Yes, you will get noticed in the daily press and they will say, "What a wonderful person." And you will get a magnificent obituary! "But God seeth the heart and that which is highly esteemed amongst men is abomination in the sight of God."

The Apostle Paul was very proud of his achievements, all he had got as Saul of Tarsus. But when he saw Christ all he could say was "I do count it but dung." "From him that hath not, shall be taken away even that which he seemeth to have." He will arrive at the bar of eternal judgment with nothing at all, just his own miserable sinful self; naked, empty, forlorn and hopeless and he will go on living like that for ever and for ever.

This word is a judgment. Have you got this vital thing or

have you not? "But what can I do?" asks someone. "I see now that I am a fool. I hadn't realised that it was a mystery. I thought I knew what Christianity is, but I see now that it means being reconciled to God, being right for the judgment and for eternity. I know nothing about it, how can I get it?"

It is quite simple. Do the opposite of what Isaiah said that these people had done. Instead of shutting your eyes in blind prejudice, open them and pay attention to the message. Come as a little child, as a pauper. Come as you are, not to criticise, not to be clever, not to justify yourself; come and acknowledge that you have nothing. "Except ye be converted," says our Lord, "and become as little children, ye shall not enter into the kingdom of heaven" (Mt 18:3). You need the simplicity of a little child. You need, in other words, an acknowledgement of your sin, of your utter failure, an acknowledgement that your great brain is of no value at all here, indeed that it has been your greatest hindrance. You have got to come saying, "I am nothing, I have nothing, God have mercy upon me a sinner." And the moment you say that, you are announcing that you have this humility, this repentance which is the essential to receiving the blessing of God in salvation and entry into the eternal kingdom of God.

6 POWER

For the kingdom of God is not in word, but in power (1 Cor 4:20).

WE ARE HERE REMINDED of another aspect of this kingdom of God that is tragically being misunderstood at the present time. This verse is a most illuminating statement, which might very well have been written at the present time and not so much to the Church at Corinth but to the church in our own country.

Look at the position as it was in Corinth. It was, of course, a Greek city and had many very intelligent citizens. It happened to be a commercial seaport, but at the same time, like all the cities of Greece, it had its academies and its porches, the places where they discussed philosophy and tried to understand the problems of life and of living. The Apostle had been there and had preached the Gospel, and a church had been established, but Paul now has to write to them because troubles had arisen in that church.

The first trouble that Paul takes up was that some of the people in Corinth had begun to criticise him. They were criticising his personal appearance; "His presence is weak," they said. They were also critical of his manner of speaking, and described it as "contemptible". As Greeks they had been accustomed to the great Greek rhetoricians, people who had studied the art of speech and of eloquence. They were experts in language and balanced their sentences; they wrote out and polished everything that they produced and they were very interested in the artistry of speaking. But the Apostle had paid no attention to things like that. He had spoken in a plain blunt manner without any art or artifice so as well as complaining about his appearance and his speech, the Corinthians said, "After all he was always talking about the same thing, about the Cross—'Jesus Christ and Him crucified'. He didn't tell us anything about the great expanse of philosophy connected with this view of his. He didn't put up the rival theories and evaluate them and then try to show the superiority of his teaching. It was all so simple, it was almost elementary; indeed, it seemed to be almost childish."

Now Paul has to write to them partly because of that. He talks about them as people who were "puffed up"; "Now some," he says in verse 18, "are puffed up, as though I would not come to you. But," he goes on, "I will come to you shortly, if the Lord will, and will know, not the speech of them which are puffed up, but the power."

That, then, was the position in Corinth. Here were these people talking and arguing so much that the Apostle has to tell them, "All right, I am ready to come. Some of you are saying that I am afraid to do so, but though I have not been able to come so far, I shall come, if it is God's will. And, when I come, I shall test you, not in terms of your speech or your words but of your power; 'for the kingdom of God is not in word, but in power'."

Now we, too, are living in an age which is very fond of discussing Christianity. Books about Christianity which shock us more and more come tumbling out one after another. They become best sellers, and the more shocking they are the more they sell, so that there is a sense in which there is a tremendous interest being taken in Christianity and the kingdom of God at the moment.

But in all the talking and the writing, and the debating and the discussions, and the symposia and the dialogues (that favourite word of today), I ask this question: where is the element of power? So let us look at what the Apostle has to say about this. He puts it in a positive form, but even his positive statement is first of all a negative. "The kingdom of God," he says, "is not in word."

Let me explain that. The kingdom of God or, if you prefer it, Christianity, the Christian message, is not just a matter of intellectual interest. That was undoubtedly uppermost in the Apostle's mind. That was the peculiar problem there at Corinth and it is still the same today. There are so many people who seem to think that the Christian message is nothing but a point of view or teaching alongside many others. There are the great philosophers, with their different schools, and amongst all these various teachings which claim to talk about man and life and death and the meaning and the purpose of existence, there is the Christian message, the Christian point of view.

So as people take up these other books and read them, so they take up the Bible and read it—or perhaps they talk more about it than they read it. But nevertheless they are interested in it as a philosophy of life. They say, "I am a seeker and a searcher after truth, I am anxious to find something that can help." So they come to this in exactly the same way as they approach all the others and they speculate and criticise and express their opinion. They read the books, they attend the lectures, they listen to the discussions and they enter into interminable arguments about Christianity—What has Christianity to say about this and about that? Is it right that Christianity should teach this and should teach that? etc. etc. The whole thing is just the view of the kingdom of God and of Christianity that reduces it to a question of intellectual interest. But the Apostle says that it is not that.

Furthermore, the Christian message is also not merely a matter for our intellectual assent only. The first group I have referred to stopped at just arguing and discussing, but I am now thinking about people who go further than that and say, "Yes, I am quite prepared to believe it, I am prepared to accept it." They adopt its creeds, if you like; they subscribe to all that it has to say and they think that that is Christianity! They have taken it up! They say they believe its teaching; some, indeed, say that they have always believed it.

But why is that not Christianity? It is for the very reason that the Apostle was saying it about these people at Corinth. They were members of the Church, and you could not be a member of the early Church unless you believed something very definitely and specifically; so these people must have been orthodox in general, whatever their criticisms were of the Apostle. But he says that the kingdom of God is not merely an intellectual assent to a number of propositions, because if it is merely that, then there is no power in it, it does not have any effect upon the life and this is a very serious thing.

There are many people who are church members and who are very zealous about their membership. They subscribe to the creeds and they like to recite them every Sunday. Some of them like to go to very early services, making sacrifices to do so, and they are full of zeal and enthusiasm with regard to the work of the church. But I have known some such people in whose lives there was no evidence whatsoever of the power of God. The Apostle elsewhere describes these people as "having a form of godliness, but denying the power thereof" (2 Tim 3:5).

And this is a terrible possibility. They have got it "in word"; they accept it, they believe it and they say they are Christians. They may even be defenders of the faith, and yet it has not influenced their lives, which may be failures. They may be failing in some obvious matters though they are perfectly orthodox. And they not only fail in their own lives, they also fail to attract others to Christianity. "I want to know, not the speech of such people," says Paul, "but the power; for the kingdom of God is not in word, but in power."

The kingdom of God, in other words, is not just a matter of a detached attitude, or of being intrigued by the Christian message. No, the kingdom of God is something that affects people, influences them, controls them and in turn makes them a power. Though the word is essential, it is not enough; there is the absolute necessity of this power, this proof, this demonstration. "I am not interested in your speech," says Paul. "Oh, I know that you are talking and saying big things and you've got wonderful criticisms. All right, but what I want to know is this: What sort of a person are you; what's your life like; what effect are you having upon other people? What do your people at home or your fellow church members think of you?"

This is a terrible thing, is it not, that you can not only believe the right things, you can be zealous about them, you can be a defender of them and you can even be tremendously keen about them, "And yet," says the Apostle, "I am not interested! Not speech but power." Now it is very important for us in our day to understand this. There is all this talk going on, but where is the power in it? What is it *doing*? And I have no doubt that this is partly the cause of the state of the churches in this country at the present time.

Let us be quite frank and honest. Towards the end of the Victorian era and during the early part of this present century, there was a great deal of "word" in the Christian Church. There was a lot of talking, much preaching, and countless books being published, but where was the power? And if you ask the man in the street he will tell you that that is why he is on the street. He got very tired of people who talked a lot about Christianity but who did not seem to practise it or to live it. They were Christians on Sunday but not on Monday and the rest of the week.

That is the criticism that the world has always brought and the world has turned its back on Christianity because it says it is nothing but a matter of words which are now out of date, outmoded and finished. "Where is your proof;" people ask, "where is your power; what are you doing; what has the Christian Church achieved?" That is the criticism and it is a perfectly fair one.

But the Apostle Paul is ready to meet it. The kingdom of God, he tells us, whatever else it may be, is a power. Let us be clear about this. The Christian message is the proclamation of, and a history of, the greatest power that has ever entered into this world. There has been nothing that has so changed and affected the life and the course of history and the lives of individuals as much as this message.

Now that is why we must always be careful to emphasise the fact that we are not concerned here primarily with a philosophy, but with a history. Jesus Christ dominates history; even the numbering of our years, 1963 and so on, is acknowledged by His birth. He is, indeed, the biggest factor and the biggest power that history has ever known. The Cross of Christ "towers o'er the wrecks of time". There is no question about this. If you merely read secular history books you will have to admit the fact that apart from everything else Christianity has been the greatest civilising influence that the world has ever known. This message literally turned the great Roman Empire, which was thoroughly pagan, into a Christian empire within three centuries! Now that is a power, not mere talk; that is not writing books, not arguing, not just being clever; that is not interchanging philosophical terms. It *did* it. And when the great Roman Empire collapsed it was this Christian Church and message that maintained what little culture was left to the world for many centuries.

The same is true of the Protestant Reformation. Whether people know it and whether they like it or not, it does not matter, but the Protestant Reformation is one of the greatest facts in our history. People boast about the Elizabethan era; about Shakespeare and other literature, and all the rest of it. But, you know, all that was the outcome of the Protestant Reformation!

Furthermore, there is no doubt but that Christianity is the greatest power, the most powerful influence that has ever entered into the life of the whole world. It has changed communities as well as changing men and women. How easy it would be to recount the story of some of the great revivals that have taken place in the history of the Christian Church. The great historian Lecky, did not hesitate to say that what saved Britain from what was experienced in France at the time of the French Revolution was the Evangelical or the so-called Methodist Revival of the eighteenth century. The effect of that revival is incalculable. It not only changed individuals but also whole communities. It gave people an interest in education, and schools came into being. It produced Sunday schools; it gave a stimulus to hospitals and medical care; it led to the reform of the poor law. All these things came out of that mighty visitation of the Spirit of God. It is a power.

So there is nothing which is so remote from the truth as to think of the kingdom of God, or of Christianity, as some sort of armchair philosophy, which you sit down and consider and argue about with others; or which some clever academics write books about to one another and create a great deal of excitement; because though they are officials and high officials in the Christian Church, they seem to be denying the very fundamentals of the Christian faith. That is not Christianity. That does nothing at all except harm and evil, whereas Christianity is a power and a power for good. It uplifts, it elevates, it emancipates. Apart from anything else, it has been the greatest civilising force that the world has ever known.

Are we clear about this? Are we clear that Christianity is primarily a power? I could recount stories of simple men preaching the Gospel in a plain and unadorned manner, and the effect of their preaching at times was to empty every single public-house in a village! There are incidents like that in the history of the Church. There was, for example, a fair that used to be held in North Wales which went on for days; it was famous for its debauchery, its drunkenness, its violence, its fighting and its evil. One sermon preached by a man called John Elias put an end to it for ever, and it has never been resurrected! That is power; that is Christianity.

Secondly, it is the power *of God*, and here is the vital point. Christianity, the kingdom of God, is not, primarily, something that we do. It does not even ask us to do anything. As the Apostle Paul puts it in Romans, "I am not ashamed of the gospel of Christ"—why? because—"it is the power of God unto salvation to every one that believeth" (Rom 1:16). It is not a message telling men to save themselves, but the power of God saving men. Take what is described in Acts 2[1]. There were the disciples, those Christians in an upper room, waiting together and praying. Suddenly, there was a "sound...as of a rushing mighty wind." And they were all filled with the Spirit and with power and they began to speak in other languages. The people around them were astonished. We are told that they talked to one another and said, "What is this? for here we are, from all parts of the world, and yet we are hearing all these people speaking in our own languages the wonderful works of God." The Christians were not saying what they had done, they were saying what had happened to them, they were bearing witness to what God had done to them. It is not our activity, it is the power of God.

This is a very basic truth. There are so many, as we have seen, who think that being a Christian means reading and talking and being interested in these things. Not at all! That is something *you* are doing. What makes you a Christian is that God does something to you. It is not that you take up Christianity, but that it takes hold of you; that a mighty power comes upon you and does something to you and turns you from what you were into something else. And because it is this power of God, it is something that affects our lives and actions profoundly; it is not just something on the surface, but something that God the Creator does and does in the depth of the soul. There is nothing greater than this "power of God unto salvation".

So that is what the Apostle means when he says, "The kingdom of God is not in word, but in power." The kingdom of God, being God's activity, His reign and rule coming amongst us, always shows itself with power because God is almighty; there is no limit to this power. He is the everlasting God, everlasting in His power as well as in all His other faculties, and the kingdom of God is nothing but a series of His actions.

The kingdom of God is always power; it is God coming and rescuing people out of the kingdom of Satan and putting them into His own kingdom and there is a wonderful picture of this in the Old Testament. There were the children of Israel, God's people, in the captivity of Egypt and they were entirely under the power and control of the mighty Pharaoh. They had no army or armaments, they had nothing. They were virtually slaves beaten by the taskmasters, urged to produce more bricks, given less straw and so on, in utter and complete hopelessness.

And the kingdom of God is that which delivered them out of it. How many times does the Old Testament tell us that story. It gives us the record historically in the book of Exodus, but the psalmists continually refer to it and recount it; and the prophets do exactly the same thing. They say that He brought them out with a mighty hand. They were helpless and the enemy was very powerful, but God came in through His servant Moses and He led them out. Read the story of the great miracles that were worked in Egypt—read about the darkness and the storm and the lightening. Then out they went and there they were before the Red Sea—Pi-hahiroth and Baal-Zephon mountains on each side, Pharaoh and his hosts behind them, the Red Sea before them. How helpless! How hopeless! But God with a mighty hand divided the sea and led them through with His almighty power. That is the kingdom of God!

And He continued to lead them in the wilderness. When there was no food He produced the manna; another time when there was no food He sent the quails; and when there was no water He made it gush out of the rock. All that is but a picture in the Old Testament of God delivering His people, God manifesting His glory, manifesting the work of His kingdom, and it is power from beginning to end. The God of thunder and of lightening, the God that can wreck an army by the word of His mouth!

But if you really want to see the kingdom of God as power, you must come to the New Testament; this is the great theme that is put before us there from the very beginning to the very end. And, of course, it is seen especially in connection with our Lord and Saviour Jesus Christ. You see it in connection with His very birth. God sent His archangel Gabriel to announce to Mary that she was going to give birth to Him, and Mary said that this is impossible because she had never known a man. But the reply of the archangel to Mary was: "The Holy Ghost shall come upon thee, and the power of the Highest shall overshadow thee: therefore also that holy thing which shall be born of thee shall be called the Son of God...For with God nothing shall be impossible" (Lk 1:35,37).

Man has been trying for many years now to produce life out of nothing but he cannot do it, it is impossible! But God can create life, so the Son of God was born without a human father! It was the power of the Almighty coming upon Mary that produced the Son of God in human form. God does not form a kingdom and save men by merely addressing words; He did that through Moses and the prophets to show that it could not be done like that. No, before God could save, He had to work a miracle and He sent His Son into the Virgin's womb! "The power of the Highest" even in His birth.

We can see this also in our Lord's teaching. The thing that impressed everybody about Him, everybody that heard Him, was this very self-same fact of power. After He had finished the Sermon on the Mount, we read that, "the people were astonished at his doctrine: For he taught them as one having authority, and not as the scribes" (Mt 7:28–29). They felt the power of His words. "Who is this?" they said, "what are these words that have such power in them? What is this man? He's never had any learning, where has He got it from?"

Even the officers of the chief priests, who were sent to arrest Him and stood and listened to Him speaking, went back and dared not touch Him. And when the authorities said, "Why haven't you brought Him?", their only answer was: "Never man spake like this man" (Jn 7:46). Everybody who heard Him was not only impressed by the graciousness of His words, but by His power, His authority and His certainty.

But the same power came out in His miracles too. There He was, apparently just a carpenter from Nazareth, Son of Mary, but He was able to heal the sick and to give sight to the blind. He could heal the deaf and the dumb. He could control the raging of the sea and silence a storm and He could drive out demons and devils. He could even raise the dead! And men and women looking at Him said, "Who is this that has authority and power even to do that?" He was not merely a teacher.

There was this demonstration of power in actions, as well as in words and He put his own emphasis upon them. One day He cast out a devil and they said, "He casteth out devils through Beelzebub, the chief of the devils." But His reply was: No, "if I with the finger of God cast out devils, no doubt the kingdom of God is come upon you" (Lk 11:15,20). And it had. Here is a power that can control the elements and can drive out diseases; there was nothing which He could not do.

But ultimately His power was manifested in the mightiest event that the universe has ever seen. Though He was so powerful, He was taken in apparent weakness and condemned after a trial which was but a mockery. They nailed Him to a tree and He died. They took down His body and they buried it in a grave and they placed a stone over the entrance. But on the morning of the third day the stone had been rolled away, and He had vanished. He had risen from the dead. He had power to overcome death and the grave. He was "declared to be the Son of God with power, according to the spirit of holiness, by the resurrection from the dead" (Rom 1:4).

Here is one who has conquered the last enemy; He has taken the sting out of death. "The kingdom of God is not in word." He is not a mere talker, a mere politician; He is not a mere "pale Galilean" teaching aesthetics. He is powerful and He conquers all enemies and speaks the Word of God. He has risen from the dead, then He ascends into heaven and, on the day of Pentecost, the Holy Ghost comes down.

We have seen how on that day the disciples were there, kneeling in prayer, when suddenly this mighty power came upon them with all its effects. When the kingdom of God comes to a man or a woman, when they enter the kingdom of God this is what happens to them. A man like the Apostle Peter, who but a few weeks before had denied Christ to save his life, once he was filled with the power he preached with boldness and attacked the very murderers of Christ without fear. He was given this boldness and utterance and power.

And what happened? Three thousand people were added to the Church! Now to be added to the Church in those days was not an easy thing. For a Jew it meant ostracism from his family; it meant being persecuted and being regarded as dead. But here three thousand were changed completely, joining the Christian Church. This is the power! And so later it was said of the Christians, "These men that have turned the world upside down have come hither also" (Acts 17:6).

No, Christianity is not just good advice, or just exhortation, it is "the power of God unto salvation" taking hold of men and changing them and putting them into the kingdom of God. Have you ever known this? Is the kingdom of God power to you or is it just a matter of words?

How, then, does this power manifest itself? The first thing it does always is to bring a conviction of sin. On the day of Pentecost when Peter preached that extraordinary sermon, the people were pricked in the heart and cried out saying: "Men and brethren, what shall we do?" It was not a mere idle word that they could argue against or be interested in or admire or dispose of as the case may be; they suddenly felt that God was speaking to them; that they had crucified the Son of God and that their hands were guilty, with the blood of Christ upon them, so they said, "What can we do? We are facing God and judgment." They were terrified, afraid of God and judgment. They were afraid of death and, alarmed, so they cried out in their agony.

Have you ever cried out like that. Have you ever known the power of conviction? Let me address a question to those who say that they are Christians. Why are you a Christian? Is it simply because you were brought up to be; is it because you think it is nice and good; is it because you have decided to take it up or because you like it as a philosophy? If so, I am not interested. Have you known the power of conviction in the Gospel; have you known anything of trembling before God and at the thought of judgment? Have you ever known yourself to be a lost soul, because that is what you are; and the preaching of this kingdom in power brings men and women to the sense of conviction of sin and of terror.

But then it is also a power that enables us to believe and to understand this message. As Paul puts it to the Corinthians: "Howbeit we speak wisdom among them that are perfect: yet not the wisdom of this world, nor of the princes of this world, that come to nought." Then speaking of the wisdom of God, he says, "Which none of the princes of this world knew: for had they known it, they would not have crucified the Lord of glory...Eye hath not seen, nor ear heard, neither have entered into the heart of man, the things which God hath prepared for them that love him." The wise men of the world regarded this as foolishness—"The natural man receiveth not the things of the Spirit of God: for they are foolishness unto him: neither can he know them, because they are spiritually discerned" (1 Cor 2:6,8–9,14). How does anyone believe, therefore? And there is only one answer. It is the power of the Holy Spirit—"But God hath revealed them unto us by his Spirit: for the Spirit searcheth all things, yea, the deep things of God." "Now we have received, not the spirit of the world, but the spirit which is of God; that we might know the things that are freely given to us of God" (1 Cor 2:10,12).

You need power to believe, to understand, to receive and to rejoice in this Word. Have you got it? That is Christianity; not just looking on in a detached manner but the power of the Word convicting and then the power to believe in Jesus Christ as the Son of God, as the Saviour of your soul, and the Spirit reveals this to you.

But Christianity is also power to create anew, to give men and women a new life, a rebirth, a new start. By nature they are lost and dead, and do what they will they cannot lift themselves up and make themselves Christian. But there is power in the kingdom of God to give new life. "If any man be in Christ," says Paul, "he is a new creature: old things are passed away; behold, all things are become new" (2 Cor 5:17). And a Christian is one who says this:

> Lord, I was dead! I could not stir
> My lifeless soul to come to Thee;

> But now, since Thou hast quickened me,
> I rise from sin's dark sepulchre.
>> William Tidd Matson

It is not that with our brilliance and our cleverness we accept this, reject that, and try to decide what God is! No, it is a power from God giving us new life, new faculties, new understanding, new everything; the power in regeneration.

But, thank God, it is also the power of God to convert us; the power that can enable us to turn from sin and from the world, from vileness and from death, to a new clean and holy life. I do not care how clever you are; I do not care how clever the books you can write are; I do not care how brilliant your jokes are against Christianity; what I am asking you is this: are you a drunkard; are you an adulterer; are you a fornicator; are you a pervert; are you falling day by day to the same sin? Your words are of no interest; that is your speech, and "the kingdom of God is not in word, but in power." Are you renewed, are you able to live a new life? That is Christianity! "Walk in the Spirit," says Paul to the Galatians, "and ye shall not fulfil the lust of the flesh" (Gal 5:16). It is not a philosophy nor is it just good advice; it is not exhortation. It comes into you as the power of a new life that will raise you up and give you power to conquer where you have failed. Many of our hymns refer to this:

> He breaks the power of cancelled sin,
> He sets the prisoner free;
> His blood can make the foulest clean
> His blood availed for me.
>> Charles Wesley

> There is power, power, wonder-working power
> In the blood of the Lamb.

This is the kingdom of God.

And it goes on, as we have seen, to give us power to face trials and tribulations in life. There is nothing that it cannot enable us to do. We can face it all and it does not matter, because "in all these things we are more than conquerors through him that loved us" (Rom 8:37).

And lastly it gives us power even to look into the face of death and to smile at it; and we go out of this world in triumph and in joy. Consider what Paul says; this is power, this is not just a talker, nor just a man who has been writing all his life. Here is a man who has known the power, so he says, "I am now ready to be offered, and the time of my departure is at hand. I have fought a good fight, I have finished my course, I have kept the faith: Henceforth there is laid up for me a crown of righteousness, which the Lord, the righteous judge, shall give me at that day: and not to me only, but unto all them also that love his appearing" (2 Tim 4:7–8).

So what about it? Have you known all this? That is Christianity; that is the kingdom of God, the power of God! Here, then, are the questions that we must ask ourselves. What of life? Do I know anything about this power of God? Is it obvious to those who live with me that the power of God is in me? Does my life show it? Are other people influenced by what they see? Can I say, "I am not ashamed of the gospel of Christ: for it is the power of God unto salvation to everyone that believeth?"

Has He made you anew? Do you know that there is a new nature in you? If not, you are not a Christian, you are outside the kingdom of God whatever your knowledge, whatever your interest may be. A Christian is a new creation born of the Spirit, born from above, born again—"not in word, but in power." Have you known this? If you have, I need not exhort you to praise God! If you have not, then go to Him; tell Him you are dead and lifeless; cry, "God have mercy upon me a sinner." And if you cry to Him genuinely, you will soon know the power lifting you out of the death and the grave of sin; putting a new life within you; leading you, guiding you, directing you, and finally receiving you into an everlasting habitation of glory!

---

[1] This sermon was preached on Whit Sunday 1963.

7 THE THREE MEN

And it came to pass, that, as they went in the way, a certain man said unto him, Lord, I will follow thee whithersoever thou goest. And Jesus said unto him, Foxes have holes, and birds of the air have nests; but the Son of man hath not where to lay his head. And he said unto another, Follow me. But he said, Lord, suffer me first to go and bury my father. Jesus said unto him, Let the dead bury their dead: but go thou and preach the kingdom of God. And another also said, Lord I will follow thee; but let me first go bid them farewell, which are at home at my house. And Jesus said unto him, No man, having put his hand to the plough, and looking back, is fit for the kingdom of God (Lk 9:57–62).

NOW I WONDER WHETHER YOU WERE SURPRISED as you read this paragraph? Here is our Lord actually discouraging a man that wants to follow Him and speaking with what appears at first sight to be real harshness to the three men. It should come as a surprise. It certainly came as a surprise to the people who heard it, to His early followers. Our Lord here seems to be behaving in a manner that is so unlike everything that we are accustomed to. We are used to the Christian Church doing everything she can to attract people, bringing great pressure upon people to come and join—and making it easy for them to do so. Here, however, our Lord seems to be doing the exact opposite. It is indeed very surprising.

But that is what we have already discovered: everything about Him is surprising. He was always doing this to people, always shocking them. This is because He is so altogether different from everything that the human race has ever produced and has ever known. But the important question for us is this: why does our Lord handle these three people in this particular way? Read again His response to each of them. Why does He speak to them in what appears to us to be a harsh and almost cruel manner? There is only one answer: He does it because He can see so clearly that they do not realise the truth of what He is saying; they do not understand His message of the kingdom. They are moved and animated by wrong motives and ideas, they are in a state of confusion and He wants them to know exactly what they are doing. That is the only explanation. Therefore, as we watch our Lord handling these three men, we can gather very valuable instruction and information concerning the nature of His kingdom, and concerning the truth as to what it means to be a Christian and how one becomes one.

Let us look back at this picture again. Here are three men who are actually following our Lord. They are in His company, they see His miracles and they are listening to Him. They are obviously interested, and yet our Lord is unhappy about them. He detects that they are all, the three of them, still in a state of fundamental ignorance about Him and about the kingdom of God. They show it in different ways, but that does not matter. And it is in order to put them right that our Lord handles the three men in this particular manner. Let us look at each of them.

Take the first: 'A certain man said unto him, Lord, I will follow thee whithersoever thou goest. And Jesus said unto him, Foxes have holes, and birds of the air have nests; but the Son of man hath not where to lay his head." What is the message here? Well, let me extract it and put it before you as a principle.

What our Lord is emphasising in His statement to this man is the importance of a right understanding of the nature of the kingdom of God. Is he not obviously a case of false enthusiasm?

He comes rushing up to our Lord and says, "Lord, I will follow thee whithersoever thou goest." He volunteers; he is ready for anything; full of keenness and excitement. "Let me come," he says, "I do not care where you go, I am going with you." He is ready to leave everything whatever the cost may be. Wonderful! And yet our Lord discourages him.

Now, do we feel, as we read this story, that this is just the kind of man that the Church needs, just the sort who makes an excellent Christian? This is the very type that, surely, should please our I ord most of all. And yet there is no question about it at all, our Lord administers a rebuff to him. He checks him and He tests him.

Why is this? Well, our Lord is able to read the minds of men and women and understands them better than they understand themselves. He is able to search the hidden recesses of the mind and the heart and to detect motives and ideas and thoughts— He recognises exactly what He is dealing with and He can see that, as he is, a man like this is no man for the kingdom of God.

Now this young man is a very common type, found today as in all ages since our Lord was here on earth. He was obviously attracted to our Lord, and by His preaching, and His miracles. This incident took place just after our Lord had performed a miracle at the foot of the Mount of Transfiguration. There was a poor boy suffering from devil-possession, a condition that was very similar, obviously, to what we now call epilepsy. The poor father of the boy, in his utter distraction and despair, had approached the disciples of our Lord while He was up on the Mount of Transfiguration with Peter and James and John. He had said, "Cannot you people do something for me? I have been hearing about this master of yours, and I have been hearing about the gifts He has given you; you have been going round and preaching and working miracles—can you heal my son?" So they had tried, and they failed. Then the father, now in a terrible condition, approached our Lord, and our Lord said, "Bring thy son hither. And as he was yet coming, the devil threw him down, and tare him. And Jesus rebuked the unclean spirit, and healed the child, and delivered him again to his father. And they were all amazed at the mighty power of God" (vs 37–43).

Now this young man had seen that, as he had seen, probably, other miracles also. He had heard our Lord's amazing preaching. There had never been a preacher like Him. The officers of the Temple, you remember, had said what was so perfectly true, "Never man spake like this man." Here was one who spoke with authority, not as the Pharisees and Scribes. He did not fumble and suppose this and think that; He just said, "I say unto you." There was an authority and a power in His preaching, and this man had heard it, and was obviously fascinated. Furthermore, our Lord was standing up, defying the Pharisees and Scribes and doctors of the law with an absolutely new teaching and this always appeals to young people. "Here is one," the man thought, "who is not one of these professionals, but who comes from the outside and puts them all in their place—He has got something new!" And so he said to our Lord, "I am coming with you! This is what I want, this is life." He was going to turn the world upside down; He was going to introduce a new order and everything would be put right: "I will follow thee whithersoever thou goest."

Is not that the picture? The picture of an idealist, of a most excellent young man who wants to do good in this world. He was starting out in life, he saw the problems and the misery and the unhappiness, and he said, "All these old people have not understood. These old fogies are all wrong. We want something new; we want a new young leader. Now here He is, so let us go after Him." And he obviously, of course, pictured a life of excitement, of wonder, of glamour and of great success.

Now I am not being unfair to him, because he had the same spirit in him as was in the disciples. Earlier in this chapter, in verse 46, we read, "Then there arose a reasoning among them, which of them should be greatest"—for it was obvious that this young Master of theirs was going to silence everybody, and then, when the time came, would undoubtedly set up His kingdom, gather an army, and become King of Israel. Then, of course, those who had been with Him were going to be given

the chief posts in His government, as it were, the most important positions. And the same thing appealed to this young
man—this new leader with His strange teaching, His wonderful power, and all the possibilities...!

This is a very common misunderstanding of the kingdom of
God even today. There are many young people who think that
Christ is just some leader like this of a popular movement that is
against the powers that be; against authority, against the failures
of the old people; something new and fresh. A movement, a
crusade, a march! And off they go with high idealism—they are
going to put the world right. I remember very well when I was a
young man listening to addresses by two preachers; both spoke
on the same subject which had been prescribed for them. It was
a religious conference, and this was a Saturday night, which was
always devoted to the young people. The subject was "The
appeal of Christ to the heroism and the enthusiasm of young
people". I did not understand very much about the Gospel
then, but I had a feeling, even then, that there was something
wrong about such a title.

You see the idea? Young people, come after Him! He will
appeal to your heroism, He will appeal to your zeal. You are
young, you have not lost your enthusiasm yet; you are prepared to sacrifice; you have the heroic note still in you; you
have not become blasé and cynical and calculating like the
middle-aged and the old. You are ready to risk, and you are
ready to follow Him.

Now the incident we are studying should have been enough
to make those conference authorities see that their subject was
quite wrong. It was because he felt that Christ was appealing to
his natural idealism and heroism that this man said, "I will
follow thee whithersoever thou goest." But our Lord's treat-
ment of him shows him that that is not the kingdom of God at
all, but something that is based on ignorance. Our Lord, in
effect, is saying to this young man, "Look here, you have got it
all wrong, you are misunderstanding what I have come to do;
and as you are," He tells him, "you are not fit to enter into my
kingdom. My kingdom is not like the kingdoms of this world.

All human movements do their best to attract followers; they appeal to them and make it easy for them; they will bribe them if necessary. All political parties do it. They want a crowd, they want support. I do not, I am different."

So He shocks him deliberately. Our Lord does not want followers, He is not interested in numbers as such. What He has come into the world to do is to save men and women and to produce new characters in a new kingdom; for we cannot enter the kingdom as we are. We may be idealistic, but it is no use here. We may be full of heroism; it is valueless. We may be full of enthusiasm; it will be damped by the Son of God. He does not want the natural man to take up His kingdom. He is the very opposite of that. Such a man has got to be changed before he can enter.

But then He goes on. "Listen," He says to this young man, "foxes have holes, and birds of the air have nests; but the Son of man hath not where to lay his head." He says, "Do you realise who I am? Do you think that I am just a popular political agitator or social reformer? Do you think I am just another man who has come to set up a movement and who is proposing to do this and that? I am not! I am the Son of man!"

Now this is His favourite title for Himself. It is a great connotation, with a profound meaning. It is another way of saying that He is the Son of God. He is the new man, the beginning of a new humanity, the start of a new race. Adam was the first man. Here is another man, the "Son of man"! A new creation is beginning. He is not merely man, He is more than man. He is *the* Man! He is God-Man!

Now this young enthusiast had not understood that. That was the trouble with all of them. They would persist in regarding Him as just a teacher amongst teachers, as they are still doing. And so they misunderstand the whole point of His teaching. "Look at me," He says, "I have not come into this world merely to teach; not merely to work miracles; not merely to create a following or to be an agitator. No," He says, "recognise who I am and that I am absolutely different. I am the Son of man, but I have neither a home, nor a house. Even the foxes have holes, and the birds of the air have nests, but I have got nothing."

So here He is, Lord of Glory, yet He has nothing! He is the paradox and the mystery. The moment you make a man of Him and put Him amongst other teachers you have lost Him. He is the enigma! God! Man! The ruler, the owner of everything! The one who has nothing! And you start by facing that most momentous fact concerning Him.

But He means more than that. We have seen how He has just healed the boy at the foot of the mount; he has shown His mastery over the elements and over every disease, and yet He says, "Let these sayings sink down into your ears; for the Son of man shall be delivered into the hands of men" (v 44).

You see, the disciples were getting a bit excited. They could see the crowds gathering round, crowds that liked the miracles and were excited by phenomena; the crowds that were interested in His discomfiture of the Pharisees and Scribes and Sadducees and doctors of the law. And there was excitement! "But," He says, "wait a minute: 'Let these things sink down into your ears.' I am going to die! I am going to be tried and condemned, I am going to die in utter helplessness and in apparent failure. Are you ready for that?"

Now that precisely, of course, is the thing that this young man had not understood at all. In his enthusiasm and excitement he wanted to be with Him, to share in this wonderful success, and to see this brilliant idealism coming into practice. "This man," he said, "will change everything. He will bring in new ideas, and He will set up His wonderful kingdom." "Oh no," says Christ, "you do not understand. I do not save men and women by teaching, by gathering armies, or by legislation. I will save them by being arrested, by being condemned, by doing nothing, by being led as a lamb to the slaughter. I save men and women by dying on a Cross! I save them by breaking my heart, by being buried in a grave, and then by rising from it! Do you accept that? No," He says to this young man, "you are too idealistic; you do not understand my kingdom. It is the opposite of what you think. It will end in apparent failure, yet in that failure I defeat the enemy, and thereby save the human race." "The Son of man is come to seek and to save that which is lost" (Lk 19:10).

Another time He put it like this: "The Son of man came not to be ministered unto, but to minister, and to give his life a ransom for many" (Mk 10:45). "If you follow me," says Christ, "you will bear the shame that I bore. Far from receiving universal adulation and applause, you will be laughed at as a fool; you will be ridiculed as one who has a religious complex. They will say to you, 'Do you believe in a Christ that died? Do you still believe in a theology of blood?' You will get scorn and derision, you will get shame and persecution—are you ready for it? You and these others are thinking about receiving the chiefest place in my kingdom; you are arguing as to which is the greatest. No," He says, "'In the world ye shall have tribulation' (Jn 16:33)—Are you ready for it?"

So there was the first man. Let us now look at the second. Here is someone whom our Lord invites to follow Him. "He said to another, Follow me. But he said, Lord, suffer me first to go and bury my father. Jesus said unto him, Let the dead bury their dead: but go thou and preach the kingdom of God." Here in a sense is the exact opposite of the first man. He was guilty of precipitancy, excitement and enthusiasm, but our Lord, looking at this second one, could see that while he was very much attracted, and interested in the teaching and in what was happening, yet he was hesitant; there was a spirit of non-committal about him and so our Lord challenged him and said, "Follow me!" And the man, you remember, responded by saying, "All right, I am coming, but 'suffer me first to go and bury my Father'."

What, then, is the principle here? Well, our Lord is teaching this man the urgency of entering the kingdom of God at once, without a moment's delay. You must be right in your understanding of it, and then you must enter it immediately. Now let us be clear about that. Our Lord's statement sounds terrible; does it not? On the surface it sounds as if He was refusing this man permission to go home to bury his poor father who was dying. But it does not mean anything of the sort. If this man's father had been ill and had died, then the son would no longer be with the Lord. The Jews were very strict about this.

No, the position was that this young man had at home an old father, who, quite conceivably, was not in good health. And so what he was really saying was this: "All right, I will come, but I cannot come now, because my father is very ill; he is old and can die almost at any moment. Let me go home and stay there until he is dead and I have buried him; then I will come and follow you."

Here, in fact, is the case of a man who says, "Yes, I am going to be a Christian, but not just now. I will be a Christian later on, when I have time. I am very busy at the moment. I am at the top of the ladder; I have great success ahead of me, I am beginning in my profession, or in my trade, or in my industry. Not yet! Oh, I like this teaching! I believe it is right; but I cannot do anything about it now."

Or he may put it in terms of age alone. He may say, "I am young now and I want to have a little enjoyment in life. Life is wonderful, it has many glittering prizes—am I going to give all these up? Why should I not sow my wild oats while am I young? Why should I not get a kick out of life? Later on, of course, when I get middle-aged or old, or when I am facing death—then is the time to think about becoming a Christian."

That is the sort of picture we have here. It is the case of men and women who can see that there is truth in the Christian message and who are troubled by it, and say—"Yes, of course that is what I really must do—but not yet." Take the prayer of St Augustine. He was not "Saint" Augustine when he prayed it; he was a brilliant philosopher, but he was troubled. He was listening to the preaching of Ambrose, that great preacher in Milan, and he was disturbed by it. He knew it was right and that he was wrong, but he was living with his mistress. Of course! And here, you see, is the fight and the conflict: he knew it was right, so he offered this prayer: "Lord make me good: but not yet."

Do you know something about that? "I want to be good but

I also want to have this other thing. 'Suffer me first…' " And how many have done this! "Let me make my name first. I do not believe in some of the things I am doing, but they have to be done, and once I have got on—then I will be a thorough Christian. I really will!" And so our Lord pulls this man up immediately and shows him that he, too, is all wrong, and He puts it in a very striking manner—"Let the dead bury their dead: but go thou and preach the kingdom of God."

What does that mean? Let me try to summarise it like this. The first thing He tells this man is that we must realise that the Gospel, this kingdom, is something which is absolutely new. He says, "If you are in my kingdom, if you are going to be a Christian, then you must realise that this is something that an ordinary man or woman cannot do. Everybody can bury the dead. You do not need to be a citizen of the kingdom of God to do that. There are people staying at home looking after their fathers who are old and dying. But that is what they are suited for, because they know nothing else and they can do nothing else. "Let the dead bury their dead." That is what the world is doing. That is the natural man and his life. He lives for this world and this life only, he knows of nothing else. He is dying, they are dying; they bury one another, they praise one another; anybody can do that and they are all doing so. But that is not the kingdom of God.

"No, the kingdom of God," He says in effect, "is for live people, not for dead ones. I am not in this world to deal with matters like that. They are all right; there is nothing wrong in a man looking after his aged parents and burying them, but, you know, that is not the first thing in life. The first thing in life is the soul! It is the life of the soul! It is the fact that men and women are not just animals who live and eat and die. No, there is a soul within them and they do not know that; the dead do not realise it. The men and women who are in my kingdom do; they are alive, awakened to the fact of the soul and its eternal destiny and its relationship to God."

"You see," says our Lord, "in a sense anybody can bury your father; but it is only a man who is a Christian who can tell your father that he has a soul that needs to be saved. 'Go thou and preach the kingdom of God.' You go and tell people about the soul; tell them that they are made in the image of God and that they have sinned and that they are under condemnation, and that if they die like that they go to hell. Awaken them! Go and tell them! They do not know it! You alone can do that, the dead cannot. You know about the soul if you understand me. I have not come to bury them! I have not come to save their bodies, but to save their souls."

"This is life! The soul needs a new life! I have come," He says, "to tell men and women that 'it is appointed unto men once to die, but after this the judgment' (Heb 9:27). I have not come into this world to reform politics or morals: that is not the business of Christianity."

Now many people are doing that. They are always talking about some recent scandals and they condemn them and talk about morals. But that is not Christianity! Christianity is here to save souls! It is an easy thing to condemn immorality. You do not need to be a Christian to do that. Many people who are not Christians do this; you can read their articles, and listen to their speeches. But that is not what Christ has come to do. Christ has come to save the immoral, to give them life anew! He has not come to do what the dead can do, He has come to do what only he who is Life itself can do! He is the Giver of life! And those who belong to His kingdom are those who realise that they have immortal souls and that they are lost, and that He alone can save them. That is the first thing.

Then, secondly, the moment you realise the truth about yourself and your soul, and the judgment of God and the possibility of hell, you do not say, "I am going to...but first let me do something else," because you know you may not have the time. The moment you realise that your soul is in terrible danger of everlasting destruction, the moment you realise the insecurity of life in this world, the moment you put these two things together, you say, "There is not a moment to be lost. I do not go back to do anything! I must be certain that my soul is saved!" You believe on Him, you enter into the kingdom;

immediately, not after doing something else. Nothing can come before this.

Is this not obvious? Our Lord Himself exemplified it. When His mother and His brothers came and tried to stop Him doing things, He rebuked them. The people came and said, "Your mother and your brethren want to see you," and He replied, "Who are my brethren? Who is my mother? These who believe in me and follow me, they are my mother and my brethren" (Mt 12:48–49). And He put it very plainly later in these tremendous words: "If any man come unto me, and hate not his father, and mother, and wife, and children, and brethren, and sisters, yea, and his own life also, he cannot be my disciple" (Lk 14:25–26).

Now our Lord does not say that as a Christian you must hate your father and mother or wife or husband. What He does say is that comparatively you have to; that He must come even before them. If your father or your mother try to stand between you and belief in Christ, put Christ first, not them; yes, even if it is your wife or husband! And if you realise the danger of your soul, you will have no need to hesitate about this, you will see that it is inevitable. You will do it at once, you cannot take the risk of being lost.

Have you seen the urgency? What is your relationship to Christianity? Is it a detachment? Are you saying, I am going— sometime—to be a Christian? If you are, you know nothing about it, you have never seen it. The message of the Lord Jesus Christ is, "Flee from the wrath to come!" Do it at once!

Finally, we come to the third and the last case. Here is another man who volunteers and says, "I will follow thee: but let me first go and bid them farewell, which are at my house." Again it seems a very reasonable request, does it not? "All right, I am coming, but I want to go home, to have a farewell party with my old friends. We have been together for years and we have had a remarkably fine time." Our Lord replies, "No man, having put his hand to the plough, and looking back, is fit for the kingdom of God."

The principle here is the importance of realising the totalitarian demands of the kingdom of God. Our Lord calls for an unconditional surrender. And once you realise the nature of His kingdom, and of what He has come to do, once you realise that it is a question of your soul's salvation, then you not only do not hesitate, you surrender unconditionally. This man was in trouble at this point, he was half-hearted. He said, "I will follow you, but I want first of all..." It is a case of divided interest and loyalty. Yes, he is going to follow Christ, but he does not want to leave the world. He wants to go with this new Master, but he would like to have just a last party with the others.

But our Lord says, "You cannot strike a straight furrow if you are looking back. It demands concentration; you must be all out. You must look ahead and do so constantly; you must never turn back again, you have finished with all that."

This is our Lord's own statement. If you want to enter this kingdom and receive its blessings and its joys, you must leave the world. You must make a clean break and turn your back irrevocably on certain things. It is a totalitarian demand. You cannot do the two things; "you cannot serve God and mammon" (Mt 6:24). "Whosoever therefore will be a friend of the world is the enemy of God" (Jas 4:4)—that is the statement of the Scripture. "Love not the world, neither the things that are in the world...the lust of the flesh, the lust of the eyes, and the pride of life" (1 Jn 2:15—16). You see it round and about you. If you love that, then you are not a citizen of the kingdom of God. You cannot mix light and darkness.

There is a terrifying illustration of this very thing in the Old Testament. It is the case of Lot's wife. Sodom and Gomorrah, where they had been living, were going to be destroyed but by the grace of God they were brought out forcibly, it was the only way of escape. And off they went, Lot and his wife and daughters, and the destruction was about to come. But "Lot's wife looked back." Why? Well, she had rather liked that life. She knew it was wrong, but she still did not want to leave it. Where were they going? To some mountain, to some wilderness. They would have to live in a cave, how miserable after the wonderful house they lived in and all the luxury! Her loyalty was divided; she looked back with longing eyes, so she was punished and became a pillar of salt (Gen 19). And it was our Lord who said to such people later on, "Remember Lot's wife!" (Lk 17:32).

Now, if you understand these things this will appeal to your logic. If you really believe that you have a soul and that it is lost; and if you believe it is lost because it conforms to the world and the flesh and the devil; if you believe that if you die like that you go to hell and spend your eternity in misery; if you believe that the Son of God has so loved you that He left the glory and the courts of Heaven and divested Himself of this glory and was born as a Babe; if you believe that He lived as a man and endured the shame, the agony, and the death, the Cross and the burial, and all that it involved—if you believe that He did all that to save you, to redeem you from the world, then can you still look with longing eyes upon the world that led to all that?

Can you still hanker after the things that ruined your soul and produced the death of the Son of God? Where is your logic? Where is your fairness? Where is your common sense?

That is what our Lord was saying to this young man; and He was saying something further. He said, "You think you want to go back to have a farewell party and then you will come after me. I know you better than you know yourself. If you go back you will so enjoy that party that you will never come after me. You start playing with it and dabbling with it, it is no good. You have seen something of what I have got, but if you have not seen the utter wrongness of all the rest and turned your back upon it and said, 'I don't want it any more', then once you go home and begin to toy with it, you will be back in the midst of it again!"

So many have said that they will be Christians "after" they have had some enjoyment. But these things do not go together, they are utterly incompatible. If you believe that the Son of God has so loved you then you will say to Him:

Love so amazing, so divine,
Demands my soul, my life, my all.
                                    Isaac Watts

I know the world has things that can sound wonderful and look very attractive, but I do not want them, I hate them, even though I know there is a hankering in me after them! But, Lord, when I see your love—

See, from His head, His hands, His feet,
Sorrow and love flow mingled down;
Did e'er such love and sorrow meet,
Or thorns compose so rich a crown?

Were the whole realm of nature mine,
That were an offering far too small;
                                    Ibid

The whole realm of nature! Yes, it is nothing by contrast with Heaven; I would give it all up! How much more would I give up the novelettes, the filthy cases in the newspaper that stimulate my evil nature and the things on radio and television that drag me down and tempt me to evil thoughts and imaginations! I will say to Him, "I am coming after you as I am! I want nothing else. You have a right to me; you have bought me with a price, I am not my own. I must glorify you in my body as well as in my spirit. I give myself to you unconditionally. You have won me, you have captivated me! I have nothing to say, except, Lord I am yours and my chief desire is to live to your glory and praise."

Fading is the worldling's pleasure,
All his boasted pomp and show;
Solid joys and lasting treasure
None but Zion's children known.
                                    John Newton

Have you learned the lessons of these three men? Have you

realised the tremendous importance of understanding the nature of His kingdom and seen the urgency of entering in without a moment's delay? Have you given yourself unreservedly unto Him, who gave Himself that you and I might live and enjoy the blessings and the glories of the Kingdom of God here in this world and for ever in the glory everlasting.

8 THE ONLY HOPE *

> Know ye not that the unrighteous shall not inherit the
> kingdom of God? Be not deceived: neither fornicators,
> nor idolaters, nor adulterers, nor effeminate, nor
> abusers of themselves with mankind, Nor thieves, nor
> covetous, nor drunkards, nor revilers, nor
> extortioners, shall inherit the kingdom of God. And
> such were some of you: but ye are washed, but ye are
> sanctified, but ye are justified in the name of the Lord
> Jesus, and by the Spirit of our God (1 Cor 6:9–11).

THERE IS NO MORE RIDICULOUS CHARGE which is
brought against the Bible than the criticism that because
it is an old book it has no longer anything to say; that
because it is old it is out of date and not relevant to the present
position; for there is nothing, if you really know your Bible,
which you will find to be more remarkable about it than that it
is always contemporary, always up to date, and always has the
exact word to say at any particular juncture or stage in the long
march and history of the human race. Take these three verses
from 1 Corinthians 6. They might very well have been written
for just this present hour, they have the very word that is
needed at this particular moment.

Indeed let me put it even further, to emphasise this point of
how contemporary the Bible always is. Those who meet here

* (See *Note To The Reader* on p. vi)

regularly on Sunday nights will know now that since the last Sunday night of April we have been considering each week the teaching of the Bible concerning the kingdom of God, and those who attend here regularly must have observed that I have been preaching to a scheme; I have had a plan and a purpose. Indeed I planned out this whole series of sermons, and the ones that are to follow for the next four weeks, during that week prior to the last Sunday in April. And according to my scheme and to my plan, I was due to preach tonight on these verses that I have just read to you. I cannot regard that as an accident, my friends. Not only is the word of God always contemporary but there is such a thing as being led by the Spirit of God.

So if you can produce any statement from any literature or any speech or anything else, anywhere in the world tonight that speaks so directly to this present moment as these verses which we are going to consider, I should be very interested to hear of them. But I know that you cannot do so. The Bible always has *the* word; it always has the last word. Why is this? It is because the Bible is what it says. It is the word of God. It is not a human book, nor a book of human theories and ideas; it is a book written by different men who all agree in telling us that they were "moved" and "carried along" by the Spirit of God. They were not writing their own opinions, they were writing what God told them to write. So it is God's revelation with respect to man and his life in this world.

In other words, the business of the Church is to preach the Bible, to unfold and expound the message of this word of God. It has been given in order that we might be taught certain things. "Know ye not?" says Paul in these verses. He expects the Corinthians to know certain things, because he had been there preaching to them, and so had Apollos. And, as a result, these people had been given information and instruction. Now that is the business of the Bible. It is to give us knowledge that is absolutely vital to our life both in this world and in the world to come.

Or, to put it another way, according to the Bible all our troubles as men and women in this world arise from one fundamental cause and that is our ignorance of certain basic, fundamental truths. We need to be taught certain things plainly and clearly; and God has given us the Bible in order that this might happen. Jesus Christ, the Son of God, came into this world for exactly the same reason. "For this cause," He says, "came I into the world that I should bear witness unto the truth" (Jn 18:37). He says also, "I am the light of the world" (Jn 8:12), and when He says that, He is saying, "I am the knowledge that the world needs. I am the only one who can enlighten men and women, the only one who can open their eyes and bring them out of darkness into knowledge." He came to teach—about God, about man, and about the way of salvation.

So the Bible gives us knowledge; and the way in which it does so is most remarkable. We have a perfect example and illustration of it in these words that we are considering. The Bible is not some kind of fairy-tale, though people think it is. They say it is "pie in the sky", that it is unrealistic. Unrealistic? It is the only Book in the world I know that is absolutely real. It is a book of facts, and of history; a book that tells us the plain unvarnished truth about ourselves. Look at the first chapter of the epistle to the Romans—what a description of life as it is! It does not spare us anything. And this passage that we are looking at here is exactly the same.

In other words, the Bible comes and it does not paint some wonderful fairy story and give us a nice feeling inside, and tell us we are all going to heaven and are all going to be happy. No, the Bible is a book that looks you in the face, examines you in the depths and tells you the truth about yourself—unvarnished—it exposes it all.

And then it proceeds to deal with the two main questions. It says, "That is life!" The newspapers boast about making revelations; they claim to examine and to give true reports; but they do not, of course. They pick out certain facts now and again but if you really want to know the truth about yourself do not go to the newspapers. They are always praising us, always playing up to us; they would not sell if they did not. The newspapers are liars about the fundamental problems of life, they do not know them, indeed they are partly the cause of the present muddle. They do not reveal the truth about man, about society and about our nation. The Bible is the only book in the world that does that. It is the only honest and truthful book. And that is, let me emphasise again, because it is the word of God.

Then, having put the facts before us in this unvarnished, almost violent manner, the Bible deals with two questions. It tells us, first of all, why things are like that. That is the first thing we want to know, is it not? It is not enough just to talk about the immorality around us; the question is, why are things as they are? So the Bible gives us the cause and the explanation of that and secondly, thank God, it tells us about the only way in which these things can be put right. Now that is the message of the whole of the Bible from Genesis to Revelation. And that is what we find, in a most extraordinary summary form, in these three verses that we are now considering.

What is it that we need to be taught? "Know ye not?" says Paul. "Are you in ignorance of these matters?" Well, the first thing that we need to learn is the terrible danger of being deceived. "Know ye not that the unrighteous shall not inherit the kingdom of God? *Be not deceived...*" The Bible warns us everywhere against this. Indeed, we can say that the case of the Bible is that man is in ignorance because he has been deceived. The whole story of the human race has gone wrong because man has been deceived by the devil.

We see this in Genesis 3. God made the world. He made it perfect; He made man perfect and put him in Paradise. And he should have lived happily; he should have enjoyed the companionship of God, and he would have been given the gift of immortality, and that would have been the story. But that is not what has happened. The story has been one of unhappiness, of jealousy, envy, murder, wars; all the horrors depicted in the Bible that we are familiar with in secular history.

So why has the history of the human race been as it has? The Bible says there is only one answer: the devil came in. We are told about the devil that he was "more subtil than any beast of the field" (Gen 3:1), and it was in his subtlety and in his deceitfulness that he deceived Adam and Eve. That is a point which is made in many places in the Holy Scriptures. Paul says in 2 Corinthians 11:2-3, "For I am jealous over you with godly jealousy: for I have espoused you to one husband, that I may present you as a chaste virgin to Christ. But I fear, lest by any means, as the serpent beguiled Eve through his subtilty, so your minds should be corrupted from the simplicity that is in Christ."

The same thing exactly is taught in the letter to the Hebrews where the writer warns his people in this way: "Exhort one another," he says, "daily, while it is called Today; lest any of you be hardened through the deceitfulness of sin" (Heb 3:13). That is always the whole cause of the trouble. And the story has been what it has, from the very dawn of history, because men and women have been deceived by the devil and by the deceitfulness of sin.

It was the trouble in the time of the Apostle Paul and in the time of our Lord Himself, who taught about the danger even of those who have listened to the Gospel being deceived by "the deceitfulness of riches" (Mt 13:22). That is the "seed sown amongst the thorns"; people are deceived by this and are kept from understanding the real meaning of life. And our Lord prophesies that it will be like that even unto the very end of the age. He says, "As it was in the days of Noah, so it shall be...As it was in the days of Lot...even thus shall it be..." (Lk 17:26-30). There it is. Deceit is the central and the most essential trouble with the human race. "Do not be deceived," says Paul, "do not be misled, do not be fooled"—and the same thing needs to be said to this modern generation.

Now there are certain particular respects in which the human race at the present time is in danger of being deceived. Let me put some of them before you. The first, as we have already seen, is the claim that the Bible cannot speak to us now because it was written two thousand and more years ago. We have learned so much since then and have advanced so much in our knowledge, so how can an old book like this speak to us any longer? It is one of the masterstrokes of the devil, that he prevents people from even reading the Bible. They will not even listen to it; they put it out of court; so they are bereft of the one message that can help them.

We are told also that the Bible does not speak to us today because we are "different". Well, what are we like? This is what they were like two thousand years ago: "fornicators, idolaters, adulterers, effeminate, abusers of themselves with mankind, thieves, covetous, drunkards, revilers, extortioners..." Are we no longer like that? There is no need to underline that, is there? The present crisis is because some of us are like that. So the Bible is speaking to men and women as they are today. They are the same as they always were. "Do not be deceived"; this book is speaking to *you*—now! It is as up to date as it was in the days of Paul.

The second aspect of deceit is to say that moral ideas change. "We do not think as our fathers used to think," people say. "We do not think as they thought a hundred years ago nor as they thought in the times of the Bible—*we* have got knowledge. What they regarded as sin we can explain biologically, or medically, or psychologically." They say, "Of course people were very ignorant and they used to condemn things...but with our new understanding, we no longer think like that."

In other words they say that morality is something relative, that there are no eternal principles and truths. What may be right for one generation is wrong for another; and what was wrong for one is right for the next. And so, for example, we are being told now that fornication is not always wrong. Sometimes it is right and a good thing, we are told; adultery is not always wrong either, sometimes it, too, may be right. Also homosexuality is no longer wrong; it can be absolutely right for certain people. Then, to tell a lie is not always wrong. If you want to show your love to your family and shield them and protect them from harm, lying may be right in such circumstances. Everything is relative; there are no eternal standards of morality and of righteousness and of truth. That is the modern teaching.

But according to the Bible that is nothing but sheer deception. You have no knowledge that entitles you to change moral canons and principles; none at all. Psychology does not answer the problem. Which school of psychology do you belong to? They are cancelling one another out, and, in a sense, they are all in the melting-pot at the moment. There is no scientific knowledge that in any way affects these moral canons. It is just man making his own laws to please himself, to excuse himself and to condone his evil. And so you get the present muddle.

But there is a third form of deceit which is, perhaps, in many ways the most serious one I have mentioned so far, and the one that, in my opinion, has been the cause of the trouble. Moral standards have been slipping and have reached their present deplorable position for one main reason—namely, that we have been taught that you can have morality without godliness. People interpret that like this: "The moral teaching of the Bible is very good," they say, "but we today cannot possibly accept its theology and its doctrines."

Now there was a man who put this very clearly, a man who was highly respected. He was a good man, I have no doubt, in a moral sense, but to me he struck at the very foundations not only of Christianity but also of morality in which he was so interested. I am referring to the late Lord Birkett, the distinguished lawyer, and this is what he said. He was being interviewed on the television and he was reminded that once upon a time he had been a Methodist local preacher. What had brought about the change? "Ah well," he said, "you know, one gets on and one learns, and one finds things out...well one does change. I no longer," he added, "believe the doctrines of Christianity. I hold on to the ethic of course. I no longer believe the doctrine but the ethic of Jesus is the highest ethic the world has ever had."

That is the teaching: that you can hold on to the ethic without the doctrines; you can have morality without godliness; and that has been the fatal teaching that has landed us in the present moral morass. People have fondly believed that you could hold on to these "good things" that are taught by Christianity, while shedding the whole basis of Christianity. The modern position is demonstrating to us in a particularly painful,

143

poignant manner that you cannot have morality without theology; that if you get rid of the doctrine then you will soon lose your morality, and as a nation we have lost it.

The fourth way in which men and women deceive themselves is to say that death is the end and that there is nothing beyond it. That is the common belief today; that when men and women die, they are finished; their life has gone, their bodies are put in a grave, and there is the end of them. But on what grounds do you say that? People say, "I no longer believe in life after death," but they cannot prove it, it is a mere assertion, a mere theory. Yet people believe it and because they believe it, they cease to worship God. But it is pure deceit. "Be not deceived!"

And then the last form of deceit is to say that God—if there is a God—is entirely love. Therefore, there is really no moral standard, no judgment, no punishment, and there is no hell. That is something that is being ridiculed of course, this idea that God is a righteous judge, who will judge the whole world at the end of time, and that some people will be punished in hell everlasting. "Out upon the suggestion!" they say. "It is impossible, it cannot be true." And they have not a vestige of proof for what they are saying. Again, it is just sheer deceit, they are being deceived by the devil.

Now, the answer to all these examples of modern deceit is given in our passage. These are the facts: "Be not deceived! Know ye not that the unrighteous shall not inherit the kingdom of God?" In other words, the answer to all this is that God *is*. That God is our maker and creator and that what matters is what He says, not what we think, and not what we think He should say. God is what He is and not what we think He ought to be. We cannot conjure up a picture of Him; we by philosophy cannot create a God. But that is what we are trying to do. Dignitaries in the Church are doing this, and I hold them, too, responsible for the present moral collapse. I am not interested in the denunciation by bishops of what may be happening at the present time when they themselves deny the essence of the Gospel.

No, you cannot separate godliness from morality, and the great statement of the Bible is that God is over all. He has made us and not we ourselves, and we are all in His hands. We say, "There are no moral standards, they are always changing." We say, "It does not matter, God is love, and all will be well." But the Bible says, "Be not deceived: the unrighteous shall not inherit the kingdom of God." That is what God says; that is what matters, and there is no excuse for our ignorance. God has revealed this to us, from the very beginning of history.

There is no need to be uncertain as to what God expects and demands of us. He has made it perfectly plain. He started off even in the Garden of Eden itself when He made this known to Adam and Eve. He said, "If you keep my commandments I will bless you; if you do not, I will turn you out." And out they went, and they have been out ever since. There is an eternal law of righteousness. God's law is an absolute law and it is in all our consciences. He has written His law in the heart of every man and woman, as well as promulgating it in an external sense as He did in the Ten Commandments.

But not only has God make it clear that there is a moral standard which He demands from us; He makes it equally clear that there is to be a judgment—"the unrighteous *shall not inherit* the kingdom of God."

Now this is just another way of saying that everybody in this world is in one of two positions; they are either in the kingdom of God or else they are not. So the question is, have you inherited the kingdom of God? All of us will have to stand before God and we will find ourselves either in the kingdom of God or else outside it. That is judgment! And, the message of the Bible is that this is the most important thing in the whole world.

It is so important, because this is what determines our ever-lasting state and condition. That is why the Apostle Paul was so anxious about these people. He says, "Do not let the devil deceive you into saying, 'I am in the kingdom of God, therefore I can drink and commit adultery and do everything I like, because God forgives me.' Oh," he says, "if you go on like that you are outside the kingdom and you are going to hell." Judgment! Damnation!

This is what the modern world no longer believes. And that is why our country is as it is. Every man is his own god, every man does what he thinks is right. Why shouldn't he? And people explain and condone it. They may in a pharisaical manner all jump on a certain man, but they are guilty of the same things themselves in their thoughts. "There is no fear of God before their eyes" (Rom 3:18). It is arrogant rebellion against God, but it is facing a God who will judge the whole world in righteousness; and the vital thing is that the judgment will send us either to heaven or to hell; it is either eternal bliss or eternal misery.

Everybody is concerned about the state of the country, but have you heard anybody talking about the state of the soul and eternal destiny? Yet that is what matters, and it matters to every one of us. Here, then, is one of the first things the Bible teaches us, this terrible, horrible danger of being deceived.

But secondly, it teaches us that nothing matters in the sight of God with respect to man but righteousness. "Know ye not that the unrighteous shall not inherit the kingdom of God?" It is not ability and cleverness: this is the vogue and the cult of clever men and women today, is it not? "He is clever," they say; "she is brilliant." No, says the Bible, not ability, not knowledge, culture, or sophistication—the "man about town", the clever people interested in art, interested in...; oh, how wonderful! Enjoyment and pleasure, money, wealth; those are the things that matter we have been told, have we not? Plenty of money, "never had it so good"! And the country has never been so bad!

No, says the Bible, in the sight of God there is only one thing that matters, and that is righteousness! Which means, if you like, character. It is not whether I am clever or lacking in ability; it is not whether I am learned or ignorant; it is not my bank balance or lack of one. Rather, it is what I am; it is my character, my soul face to face with God. Righteousness! both in a nation or in an individual is the only thing that matters with

Him. "Righteousness exalteth a nation' (Prov 14:34). "Where there is no vision the people perish" (Prov 29:18), though they may have been great and though they sing the glories of the past. Where people live for sport and pleasure and money and getting on and cleverness, but "where there is no vision", then "the people perish". Rome perished and others have perished since.

So nothing matters in God's sight but just this matter of righteousness. He revealed it in the garden of Eden, and in the Ten Commandments. His own people have always realised this. The Psalmist says, "Who shall ascend into the hill of the Lord? or who shall stand in his holy place? He that hath clean hands, and a pure heart" (Ps 24:3–4). Not your clever fellow, not your brilliant men and women of affairs, not those who can speak cleverly, your sophisticated, modern people. No! Clean hands! A pure heart! That is what God wants.

David understood that. He said in another place, "Thou desirest truth in the inward parts" (Ps 51:6). Yes, says our Lord, "Except your righteousness shall exceed the righteousness of the scribes and Pharisees, ye shall in no case enter into the kingdom of God" (Mt 5:20). He says it again: "Ye are they which justify yourselves before men; but God knoweth your hearts: for that which is highly esteemed among men is abomination in the sight of God" (Lk 16:15). You get on, you are a Cabinet Minister, you are praised by men—but "highly esteemed among men is abomination in the sight of God." Righteousness!

Men and women were meant to live as God made them to live. They were meant to live to His glory and to keep His commandments. They were meant to be upright; to be pure and clean and honest and noble. They were put on their feet so that they might look into the face of God and enjoy His companionship. That is righteousness.

But the Bible goes on to tell us that we are all unrighteous by nature. "There is none righteous, no, not one" (Rom 3:10). In spite of all the divisions into class and education and money and all these other things, all are unrighteous. Unrighteousness takes different forms. We are not all guilty in detail of these particular sins, but we are all sinners. There are many people in this land tonight who are guilty of these very sins that are mentioned in the list of our text. However, the fact that you may not be does not mean that you are righteous. To be righteous means that you love the Lord your God with all your heart and all your soul and all your mind and all your strength; and that you love your neighbour as yourself. So are you righteous? Are you living to the glory of God and to His praise? That is righteousness! But none are righteous; "All," says the Apostle Paul, "have sinned and come short of the glory of God" (Rom 3:23).

What is the cause of this? The Bible tells us, and this is the vital message. Every one of us born into this world is unrighteous because man fell from God. Adam was righteous until he listened to the devil; then he fell and became unrighteous. And man is unrighteous still because he has turned his back upon God. He is a rebel against Him and has become the slave of the devil, and of these lusts and passions. He becomes debased, depraved, and a miserable slave. So that is the second great thing that is taught us in the Bible, and we have already considered this in our earlier studies—that nothing matters in the presence of God but righteousness. And there we see ourselves all condemned, all sinners, and all unrighteous.

But, thank God, the Gospel does not stop there. It tells us all this, and we need to know it. Let us look at these words again: "Be not deceived: no unrighteous person shall inherit the kingdom of God: neither fornicators, nor idolaters, nor adulterers, nor effeminate, nor abusers of themselves with mankind, nor thieves, nor covetous, nor drunkards, nor revilers, nor extortioners, shall inherit the kingdom of God. And such were some of you. *But...*"—and here is the essential message of the Gospel—"but ye are washed, but ye are sanctified, but ye are justified in the name of the Lord Jesus, and by the Spirit of our God."

What, then, has the Gospel got to say about this deplorable state in which we find ourselves as a nation at this moment?

And it is not only true of this nation, it is true of all the nations. What is the message? Well, it is not a mere message of denunciation of sin and of the sinner. You do not need to be a Christian to do that. Moral men and women are holding up their hands in horror tonight. They are not Christians, but they are moral people, and they are denouncing it.

Neither is the message of the Church merely one of exhortation or of appeal. I read the other day of a church dignitary saying that we must "clean up the stables". And all the leaders are expressing their opinions upon "this moral degeneracy" and so on. But that is nothing but pharisaism! Our Lord has dealt with that once and for ever, in the incident that is described to us at the beginning of the eighth chapter of John's gospel. They brought a woman to Him who had been caught in the very act of adultery. They rushed her into His presence, and wanted to know what His verdict was on the case. And He, instead of answering them, began to write on the ground. But they were pressing Him, so He looked at them and said, "He that is without sin among you, let him first cast a stone at her" (v 7). And they all slunk out as quietly and as quickly as they could, leaving the woman and her blessed Lord together alone.

Be careful what you are doing, my friend. It is a very simple thing to point a finger of scorn at a man, and to condemn him. But what of you? Is your heart clean? Are your hands clean? Be careful! Examine yourself! It is an easy thing to make scapegoats. I am not defending any wrong doing; there is no defence of sin. But I would emphasise that the Gospel does not merely denounce it, nor does it merely make a moral appeal. We shall hear a lot of that in the future. We shall hear great appeals to the nation to pull together, and we are going to put up a show of being Christian again. It is of no value, it is sham.

Nor is it just an appeal for more moral education or any other form of education. Many people believe that education is the solution to all our problems. A political leader said recently, "The strength of a nation depends upon its education. Education is the key to unlock the storehouse of the future." But education, though it is a good thing, is not enough. It is often the best educated people who are some of the ringleaders in vice and evil and who can sink to such deplorable levels.

Nor is it the Gospel message merely to tell men and women to believe in Christ and to say, "Lord, Lord!" and then say that everything is all right. That is the very thing against which Paul is warning the Corinthians. Here were these members of the church at Corinth and yet some of them were guilty of foul and terrible sins, which he has mentioned in the fifth chapter. And they thought they were all right because they believed in Christ. And there are many such people today, too many by far in our churches. They say, "I took my decision for Christ, I gave myself to Him" and they think that that puts them right, they can live as they like. But that is antinomianism—living in sin, living in dishonesty, living carelessly and saying, "Lord, Lord!" It does not work. "The unrighteous shall not inherit the kingdom of God." No, merely to say that you believe is not enough, that is not the Gospel.

I am afraid, however, that we shall see a good deal of this. We shall have some kind of moral cleansing; and people will attend services and will be told in the Press that Cabinet Ministers are attending services and people are showing an interest in religion. But if it is not a change in heart, it is a lie, it is deceit again. Even an attendance at the house of God is not enough, though it is a good and an excellent thing in itself.

What is the message of the Gospel then? Well, thank God it is here in this passage. It is a message of salvation. We do not denounce sinners, we save them. We do not point a finger of scorn at them like a Pharisee. We go to them and say, "You can be delivered out of this, you can be washed, you can be cleansed and renewed, you can be justified in the name of the Lord Jesus." It is a message of hope, a message of salvation. But let us make sure that we have the message of the New Testament, the old, old, Gospel, this plain, unvarnished word! It gives a hope for the vilest, because it does not merely appeal to men and women to pull themselves together; it tells them that God will take hold of them. "It is the power of God unto salvation to every one that believeth" (Rom 1:16). It is a message that comes to men and women in the depths of degradation and sin and evil, and tells them that they can be converted, that they can be saved, that they can be renewed. Look again at that list of sins in our passage. "That is what you were!" says Paul. 'But you are no longer that. Why? Oh, because you have been washed—you have not done it—you have been sanctified, you have been justified in the name of the Lord Jesus, and by the power of our God.'

I am privileged to preach a Gospel that can wash us from the filth of sin, a Gospel that can cleanse us and purify us from the pollution of sin, a Gospel that can absolve us from its guilt and give us a robe of righteousness to stand in the presence of our holy God. This is a Gospel that not only preaches forgiveness; it preaches renewal, a rebirth, a regeneration. It preaches that a new man or woman can rise out of the ashes of the failure and walk as a saint before God.

How does it happen? Paul answers the question—"in the name of the Lord Jesus, and by the Spirit of our God." The Christian message is that the Son of God, the Lord Jesus Christ, came out of heaven into this world in order to save us. He did not come merely to teach us and to exhort us, to condemn our sin and to say, "This is how to live, follow me." He knew we could not. Here we are, guilty of lusts and passions—slaves! And we are all slaves to something. Is there not something that gets you down? Do you not feel ashamed as we consider these things? What of that sin which you keep on repeating? Why do you not stop it? You are a slave to it, that is why. It may not be adultery but it may be jealousy and envy and malice and spite and hatred, or an inordinate ambition and pride in the things of this world. And it is the power of God alone that can save us.

So He came to reconcile us to God. We are guilty before God, and how can we have communion with Him and how can we be blessed when we are guilty? I cannot undo my past, I cannot live the law, so what can I do? Christ came and He has done it for me! He became man, He put Himself under the law, He has kept it, He has borne my sins in His own body on the tree, He has been smitten for me! And in Him God forgives me

151

and He takes His righteousness and puts it on me. "…justified in the name of the Lord Jesus!"

Adulterers or fornicators, or liars, or murderers, or even perverts of the worst type, when they believe in the Lord Jesus Christ they are delivered, they are washed, they are justified, they are sanctified! The Christ of God has come to deliver them, to lift them out and to set them upon their feet and establish their goings. I am not here to denounce a poor man who is a sinner like I am! I am here to tell him—if he could hear my words and God grant that he may—that he can be delivered, he can be pardoned, he can be renewed, he can start a new life in Jesus Christ.

That is the Christian message! Not your pharisaism, not your decency and pretence and play-acting at religion, but entirely new men and women, with righteousness in their hearts and the righteousness of Christ upon them, living to the glory of God—born again. And it is all possible because the Lord Jesus Christ the Son of God came from heaven and died on that cross. Here is the Gospel! Thank God it is! We do not merely point fingers and condemn. We do condemn, but we wound in order to heal, we knock down in order to lift up. We show men their guilt and their helplessness and their hopelessness and their woe, that they may submit to the power of God unto salvation through Jesus Christ our Lord, and by the Spirit of our God.

And so, what of you? Are you righteous? Are you ready to stand in the presence of God at the bar of eternal judgment? Are you living a righteous and a holy life? Are you clean? Are your hands and your heart clean? Is your mind or your imagination clean? Forget everybody else, start with yourself, and realise that you, too, need to be washed and sanctified. Can you use the words that were written by William Cowper—

> The dying thief rejoiced to see
> That fountain in his day;
> And there have I, though vile as he,
> Washed all my sins away.

Have you? Have you seen this message, and are you ready to say—

> I hear Thy welcome voice
> That calls me, Lord, to Thee,
> For cleansing in Thy precious blood
> That flowed on Calvary.
>   Lewis Hartsough

If you have not realised your own need of cleansing, you are in no position to point a finger at somebody else. If you have not seen that nothing but the blood of Christ can cleanse you from the guilt and power of sin, then you are not a Christian, you are a miserable self-righteous Pharisee. See your own blackness and pollution, turn to Him and say,

> I am coming, Lord,
> Coming now to Thee:
> Wash me, cleanse me, in the blood
> That flowed on Calvary.

And, you know, when you are washed and when you are cleansed you will have some sympathy with fallen men and women. You will not make a sensation of such cases and talk self-righteously; you will be sorry for them, you will pray for them, you will want to tell them the message, so that they can be delivered. Why do they live this filthy life? It is because they do not know of a better one. It is because they are ignorant of the Gospel. It is because they are being deceived by the devil and by modern learning, often preached by the Christian Church herself.

And the only people who can help moral failures in this world, and be of any value in society at this moment, are men and women who, having realised their own impurity, and their own utter hopelessness, have turned to Him and have said—

> Rock of ages, cleft for me,
> Let me hide myself in Thee;
> Let the water and the blood,
> From Thy riven side which flowed,
> Be of sin the double cure,
> Cleanse me from its guilt and power.
>
> Augustus Toplady

And He has washed and cleansed them, and they can tell others that they have but to do the same thing, and they will know the moral, spiritual cleansing that the Son of God alone can give, and the new walk and the new life which the Holy Spirit of God alone can enable one to walk. "But ye are washed, but ye are sanctified, but ye are justified in the Name of the Lord Jesus, and by the Spirit of our God."

Thank God, in spite of our present position there is a hope tonight! It is the only hope. It is the Gospel of Jesus Christ and Him crucified! Do you know Him? Are you resting upon Him? Have you been washed and cleansed and renewed by Him?

9 TRUE RICHES

Jesus looked around, and saith unto his disciples,
How hardly shall they that have riches enter into the
kingdom of God! And the disciples were astonished at
his words. But Jesus answered again, and saith unto
them, Children, how hard is it for them that trust in
riches to enter into the kingdom of God! It is easier
for a camel to go through the eye of a needle, than for
a rich man to enter into the kingdom of God (Mk
10:23–25).

IN THESE WORDS OUR LORD COMMENTS on the case of the
rich young ruler who had just turned his back against Him
and gone away from him grieved and sorrowful. Now we
have already seen how the various difficulties about the kingdom—the misconceptions concerning its nature and character
and what one has to do in order to enter it—how they contradict one another and are almost poles apart, and yet they are all
in trouble.

Here again we see the same thing. We have just considered
that statement of the Apostle Paul in 1 Corinthians 6:9: "The
unrighteous shall not inherit the kingdom of God", and we saw
that that is a message that is needed very badly in our society.
People seem to think that the kingdom of God just announces
that God is love. You can do anything you like—break your
vows, be dishonest and unfaithful to your marriage vows—it

does not matter, the love of God is going to put you all right at the end. "Be not deceived," says Paul. Badness is not allowed in the kingdom of God. But now, in these verses, we find the exact opposite. Badness excludes us, yes, but the point here is that goodness is not enough. For that is the major element, it seems to me, in the particular case of this, so-called, "rich young ruler".

This is, in many ways perhaps, the peculiar fallacy of this present age. I believe one of the main troubles today is that people have got hold of the idea that the one thing that is necessary for us to enter into the kingdom of God and to be all right with God is to be good. Goodness is the key. People are no longer interested in doctrine, they tell us, they abominate theology. "Ugh!" they say, "'The fathers taught...' what does it matter? As long as we are good people and live a good life and so on, surely that is all that God demands."

And so you get these people who talk about holding on to the Christian ethic though they have dropped the doctrine; or those who say, "I never go to a place of worship, of course, but I am living the Christian life, I trust." I read once about a man who said of his father, "He was the finest Christian I ever knew; though, of course," he added, "he did not believe any of the Christian teaching." And so people who never come to worship God, and who are not interested in the Christian faith and the doctrine of the faith, regard themselves as good Christians because they are good men and women.

Now this particular story deals with this in a final and in an exhaustive manner. The case of the rich young ruler is extraordinary and it is also grievously misunderstood. There are many who think that this is a specific message to rich people. This was one of the favourite texts of the people who used to talk such a lot about Christian Socialism in the early years of this present century. Many still do so, and here, they think, is their one text; the rich man is condemned, and, therefore, all who are not rich are all right. But, of course, that is a complete misunderstanding of the whole incident and its teaching. This is a message for every single one of us. It speaks directly to our particular case whatever it may be at this moment; it applies to us all.

It is, of course, one of the most surprising cases in the New Testament. Of all the people who ever came to our Lord, there is no story that is so surprising to the non-Christian as that of the rich young ruler. You would have thought that this was just the type of man that our Lord delighted in and that He wanted to see coming to Him. You would have presumed that this of all men was one who would have received an open-armed welcome, and who would have gone without any difficulty into the kingdom. He was such an excellent young man, and yet, you see, he went away sorrowful.

According to the modern view, then, here is almost a perfect Christian, and yet he is outside the kingdom. This is astonishing and, indeed, we are told that the disciples themselves in their misunderstanding of the kingdom really could not take it. Verse 26 tells us, "And they were astonished out of measure, saying among themselves, Who then can be saved?" When they saw this young man going away and our Lord's comment upon it, the disciples could not understand this. They said, "Isn't he in the kingdom? If he is not, then who can be in? This seems impossible."

So here again I want to emphasise that the kingdom of God is entirely different from everything that the natural man has ever thought about it. The first thing we must do if we want to enter this kingdom is to shed all our preconceived notions and ideas; to get rid of all our own thoughts and submit ourselves with humility and as little children to the teaching of our blessed Lord Himself.

This is the first principle. We all think we know what a Christian is and what we must do to enter the kingdom of God, and so we all think that this is *the* thing. The disciples thought that. But our Lord showed them that they were altogether wrong. That is why this young man is such an important case. Look at him; how well he starts! He always reminds me of typical English weather—it starts with glorious sunshine in the morning and you think you are in for a wonderful day, but it ends in a storm. Who could have started better than this man? He had been living a very good and moral life. And yet, the best thing of all about him, in a sense, is that he was conscious of the fact that he needed something more, something further. "Good Master," he said, "what shall I do that I may inherit eternal life?" Though he was so noble, so excellent, he was not satisfied.

Now there are so many who are not conscious of this further need. They are self-satisfied, self-contained. That was the trouble with most of the Pharisees. They just went before God and said, "I thank Thee, O God, that I am not as other people are, indeed that I am as I am"! Not so this young man! "What shall I do that I may inherit eternal life?"

I sometimes think that perhaps what had brought him to that realisation was that he had been listening to our Lord and following him. And from the moment he had met Him and listened to Him be began to feel a sense of dissatisfaction. He was better than most people but here was something bigger, something greater. Our Lord exposed some need, so the young man was concerned about the satisfaction of this further need. He had not got eternal life and he wanted to know how to get it—and you cannot say anything better about a natural man than that.

But beyond that, he did something about it. He came to our Lord, and you notice the way in which he approached: "And when he was gone forth into the way, there came one running"—look at his eagerness and his zeal. He did not say, "Oh well, I can go and listen to Him again." No, this thing had become a big problem to him and he ran.

Then you notice, too, his manner of approaching our Lord: "he kneeled to him". He showed Him respect; he showed that he admired Him and was aware of the fact that here was no ordinary Teacher, but that there was something extraordinary and exceptional about Him. And so he wanted to learn from Christ, and he put the right question to Him—this question about "eternal life". Things were very good for him in this life, but he said, "What shall I do that I may inherit eternal life?" You cannot imagine a better question than that.

And, indeed, to cap it all, and to prove that my understanding of the man is right, we are told this: "And Jesus beholding him loved him." Our Lord liked his question, and his whole attitude. What an excellent start! Would you not anticipate that the man would go straight into the kingdom without any difficulty? But that is not the story—"And he was sad at that saying, and went away grieved: for he had great possessions."

So what was the matter with this young man? Why did he go away, why did he not enter the Kingdom? What was the trouble? Our Lord answered these questions in this comment: "Jesus looked round about, and saith unto his disciples, How hardly shall they that have riches enter into the kingdom of God!…Children, how hard is it for them that trust in riches to enter into the kingdom of God!" It was nothing but his profound misunderstanding of the kingdom of God that sent this young man away disappointed and unhappy: "he went away grieved", wounded in spirit, "sad at that saying".

Now before I proceed to the analysis and to discover with you why it was that he went away like this, let me ask a simple and an obvious question: what has been the result of *your* coming to Christ to listen to Him? What is your reaction to the Gospel of the kingdom? According to this teaching in the New Testament there are, ultimately, only two reactions; one is that you are so captivated by it that you immediately enter, or else that you are grieved by it and offended by it.

Here is a young man who was "grieved" at what Christ had said; he was annoyed and "sad at heart" and he went away sorrowful. Do you know anything about that? What has Christ done to you? You are bound to react to Him in one way or another. If you have never reacted to Him at all, it is because you have never come near Him. You can sit in churches and listen to sermons and read Bibles and yet never meet Him, but when you do meet Him you must have one of those two inevitable reactions.

Has Christ ever upset you? Have you come into such intimate contact with Him that He has annoyed and offended you? The Apostle Paul talks about "the offence of the Cross" (Gal 5:11), and I feel sometimes that the trouble with so many today is that the Cross means nothing to them, it does not even annoy them, it is not an offence to them. But there is something about this blessed Person. He is either everything to you or else He is an offence to you and you go away grieved and sorrowing. You cannot be indifferent to Him, you cannot just look on and remain exactly the same at the end as you are at the beginning. I would sooner see men and women annoyed by Him and offended by Him than feel nothing about Him; because there is hope sometimes with people who are offended. They may be touched and convicted; they may even be wounded, and they will come back; they will have to come back and they want more. But what is impossible is sheer indifference; it means they have never seen Him, they have never met Him. But this young man was grieved and went away sorrowful. Why?

Let me answer that question in the form of three principles. The first is that he went away like that because of what Christ did not say to him. Now that is odd, but it is very true in this case. The young man made it quite obvious that he came to our Lord expecting Him to say certain things, expecting Him to give a particular answer to his question. "Good Master," he says, "what shall I do that I may inherit eternal life?" He expected Christ to confirm his ideas. He had been listening to Him, and he had worked it all out, so he came and put his question expecting a certain answer. We can all do that; we all come to Christ and become concerned about the kingdom of God with our preconceived notions and ideas, and we come to Him for confirmation. But the young man did not get it. Our Lord did not say to him what he had anticipated and it is one of the reasons why he went away.

But that is putting it generally—let me divide that up. He expected our Lord to say, "Quite right. I can see you are very good; I can diagnose you; I can more or less tell your position by looking at you. It is all right as far as you have gone, but you have not gone quite far enough. There is just another good work you have not thought of, but it is easily within your competence. So go and do it. You just need to add this thing, this one extra something to what you have got and then you will be in the kingdom." But He did not say that. He never says that. That, undoubtedly, was Nicodemus's fallacy. Nicodemus had got this same notion—"I am a master of Israel, this man has got something I have not got, and I want this something extra." We all think that Christianity is something we add on to our lives; but it never is. There is something explosive about it—it smashes all we have got. This young man was smashed; our Lord demolished him!

No, it is not a matter of simple arithmetic, simply adding to what you have got. It is altogether different; it means being "born again", starting afresh. All you have is useless; your righteousness is as "filthy rags". You do not add on, you receive it all.

Secondly, the young man was expecting our Lord to tell him to do something that he could do with comparative ease. "Good Master," he said, "what shall I do that I may inherit eternal life?" There he was, attracted by our Lord, a good, idealistic young man, thoughtful, moral and concerned about the uplift of life and the improvement of the race—"Tell me," he said, "I am ready, what do you want me to do?" And what he was told was that what he needed to do is something that he would not do; he was told that entry into the kingdom was beyond his capacity— "with man it is impossible; but not with God: for with God all things are possible."

This is the fatal fallacy, it runs through the whole of the Scripture, that men and women can earn their salvation and make themselves Christians; that by striving they can enter the kingdom of God, and make themselves children of God. But here comes a blank "No!" Our Lord gives a denial, as it were, to this self-confidence and assurance which people have in their own ability to please God and to make themselves righteous. The young man was offended by what our Lord did *not* say.

But let me go on to something more positive and more important. He was offended and went away sorrowful because of what Christ *did* say, and this is our next principle. Our Lord told this young man, as plainly as words can ever put it, that morality and goodness are not enough. "Jesus said unto him, Why callest thou me good? there is none good but one, that is God. Thou knowest the commandments"—of course you do, I can tell by looking at you. You are a learned young man, and religious, and you have paid great attention to the teaching of the Law—"Thou knowest the commandments, Do not commit adultery, Do not kill, Do not steal, Do not bear false witness, Defraud not, Honour thy father and mother." Those, you see, are the Commandments, the second table of the Law—and oh! how they are needed at the present time, for they are still the commands of God.

Then the young man answered and said, "Master, all these have I observed from my youth." "Of course I agree," he said in effect, "you are right, and this is the kind of life I have been living. I have never done anything else. I have always obeyed those Commandments. All is well, therefore, isn't it?"

Here is the reply to that: "Jesus beholding him loved him, and said unto him, One thing thou lackest:"—It is not enough; you can keep the Commandments but still it does not put you in the kingdom. You can keep these—it was the second table only, remember, He had not mentioned the first—but you can be right on these and still you do not go in. This is the modern position: is it not? A good moral man living a clean life, out to improve the lot of the race, making sacrifices—ah! the finest type of Christian! "No," says Christ, "morality and goodness are not enough. They do not admit one into the kingdom of God."

But the second point under this second heading is this, and here we come to the heart of the matter. The young man went away sorrowful because Christ told him the simple plain and unvarnished truth about himself. He went away sorrowful because Christ told him the real trouble in his life. Here is the thing that always cuts and hurts and offends. Here we see, standing out, the tremendous understanding of human nature that our blessed Lord had. You remember how John in his gospel gives us a most interesting word about Him, "Now when he was in Jerusalem at the passover, in the feast day, many believed in his name, when they saw the miracles which he did. But Jesus did not commit himself unto them, because he knew all men, and needed not that nay should testify of man: for *he knew what was in man*" (Jn 2:23–25). And here is the rich young ruler, this noble young man standing before Him; our Lord reads right into the depth and centre of his being and exposes to him his real trouble and his real need.

Here is the principle. We all think that we know what we need, that we are experts at diagnosing ourselves and our own case. We say, "Well I am doing this and that, but it is not enough; what I need is further light, further knowledge, or further understanding. I am still not quite right; I am not quite happy, I have not got a full intellectual understanding of that odd point of theology, that is my trouble. I do not see how a God of love can be a God who punishes at the same time; I cannot quite get this idea of atonement, of one dying for another; it does not seem to me to be quite moral. My difficulties are intellectual you see. So I come to Christ in order to get the resolution of my intellectual problems, questions and difficulties." That is how we talk to ourselves is it not?

This young man went to Him in that spirit. But he had come to one who reads us like an open book; to one who knows us better than we know ourselves; he came to one who penetrates behind all the sham and the pretence and the camouflage with which we delude ourselves and all we fool others with—He sees to the heart of the problem and He exposes it to us and that is the thing that kills. He did it with this young man: "Jesus beholding him loved him, and said unto him, One thing thou lackest: go thy way, sell whatsoever thou hast, and give to the poor, and thou shalt receive treasure in heaven: and come, take up thy cross, and follow me." That was the thing that did it!

Now in this particular man's case the trouble was his riches. There is no doubt about that at all. But you notice it was not the riches as such. Our Lord makes that quite clear. "How hardly shall they that have riches enter into the kingdom of God! The disciples were astonished at His words. But Jesus answered again, and saith unto them, Children, how hard is it for them that *trust in* riches to enter into the kingdom of God!"

In other words, the trouble with this young man was not merely that he was a wealthy young man; it is not a question of riches, but of pride in riches, of confidence in them. The trouble with this young man was the power of money, what he could do with it, and what he could bring to pass through it. Money is power, and this young man knew it. That is why a rich man is in a very dangerous position; because the trouble with all of us ultimately is that we desire power.

But it is not only money; it is equally bad when it is pride of intellect, power of mind, or power of speech, any power is always dangerous. All power corrupts. Here it happens to be the power of money, because with his money he could do such a lot of good and he was a man who liked doing good; but he liked to do it in his time and in his way—it gave him great self-satisfaction. Do not misunderstand him; he really did a lot of good with his money, but it was *he* who was doing it, with self-satisfaction and pride, and he wanted to keep his hand on the wealth. "Give it away," says Christ, "and let me decide."

For it was not merely the money, but his attitude to it, his reliance upon it, his trust in it. I have no doubt that, partly, it came from the enjoyment of what money can buy—the food and the companions and the fellowship, and the comforts of life and all these things—but the essence of it was just that, that he was in charge and in control of his money and what he could do with his wealth.

But let us not imagine that our Lord was only talking about money. We are all holding on to something, taking pride in something, and that is the thing that constitutes the obstacle to our entry into the kingdom of God. It may not be wealth in your case, indeed, we do not hear so much about this story being used against rich people at the present time because of the great levelling process that is taking place in this country. And in the old days even the trouble with the poor man was that he wanted to be rich; his objection was not to riches but that the other man had them and not he. The poor man has often been as covetous as the rich man; how we fool ourselves in this respect!

But it is not only a question of money. We come to Christ, we are interested in religion, we want help, we say, we want this knowledge, this understanding. We think we need intellectual understanding but that is not what we need at all; and here our Lord speaks to this present generation. They are trying to make us think that the trouble with religion is intellectual; that is why they are writing all these books. They say, "It is no use preaching that old Gospel in this scientific, educated age. People will not accept it. You must give them a message that will appeal to their intellects and to their understanding. So we must reconstruct the faith and start anew and produce a gospel for modern men and women."

And here is the final answer to that from the Son of God Himself. He says, "No, the problem is not intellectual, it is moral." It is always moral. The difficulty about the kingdom of God is never intellectual. This is the camouflage we put up, the false problem that we think is troubling us, this is the false question that we ask. But we are concealing something and Christ with His penetration gets through it all. He says, "Here is your trouble; it is this pride of money, your reliance upon it, the power that it is giving you—that is the thing you are proud of. It is not these questions you are asking me—'Go thy way, sell whatsoever thou hast'." And that is why the young man went away sorrowful; Christ had exposed the trouble, he had convicted the man of his essential sin. And He always does that.

Has He put His finger on your particular sin? If you cannot say "Yes" it means that you have never met Him. This is the startling thing: we come with our intellectual problems, and so on, or we think we need a little help here or there. "No!" He says, "that is not your trouble, it is that lust that is controlling you; lust of money, lust of power, physical lust, sexual lust, whatever it is." He comes straight to the centre, and you are held face to face with yourself and the running sore of your soul.

Then the third reason why the young man went away is that

Christ said unequivocally that the kingdom of God must be entered in His way and in nobody else's. So He issued a categorical imperative and made a totalitarian request: "Go.. sell all that thou hast, give to the poor, and come...".

This is a fundamental principle of this Gospel of salvation. He decides how we enter the kingdom, we do not. We just submit and obey and follow Him. We just make an absolute surrender to Him. It is not our idea, it is His. And that is where the offence comes in. "The young man went away grieved and sorrowful." Why? "Well," he said, "I thought that the way into the kingdom was to do the things I have already done and to add something to them. I was ready to do it and I believe I could have done it; but," he said, "He made an impossible request. I cannot do that, this is monstrous."

For "the preaching of the cross is to them that perish foolishness; but unto us which are saved it is the power of God...For the Jews require a sign, and the Greeks seek after wisdom: But we preach Christ crucified, unto the Jews a stumblingblock, and unto the Greeks foolishness" (1 Cor 1:18,22– 23). They will not have the Cross! The offence and the hatefulness of the Cross. But it is there; He says there is no other way. You must come this way. Your intellect has got to be humbled, your pride has got to be put down; you must come as a little child. You must enter in and there is only one way into the kingdom, Jesus Christ and Him crucified. And men and women hate it, and object to it. They say, "I believe in, I like Jesus, I admire His person, I like His teaching. The Sermon on the Mount to me is wonderful; I like His ethic and admire it. But when you tell me that I have got to believe that He died for me, that He bore my punishment, it is monstrous, it is immoral, I cannot, I will not...!" And away they go offended by the most glorious thing of all, as this young man went away.

But it is our Lord who decides, not you and not I. "I determined," says Paul, "not to know anything among you save Jesus Christ and him crucified" (1 Cor 2:2). "Other foundation can no man lay than that is laid, which is Christ Jesus" (1 Cor 3:11). "I am the way, the truth and the life: no man cometh unto the Father, but by me" (Jn 14:6). "The Son of man came not to be ministered unto, but to minister, and to give his life a ransom for many" (Mt 20:28). It is the only way, but this young man could not submit to it, so he went away sorrowful.

And then there is, finally, this call to follow Him, this allegiance that He demands. "Come," He says, "after you have given away all the proceeds of the sale, 'take up the cross and follow me'." This does not mean that you enter into the highest intellectual circles of respectability, nor that you will get all the plaudits and the applause of men. No, rather, it means that you take up your cross. It may mean separation from your nearest and dearest; as He has just been saying earlier in the chapter; it may mean leaving father, mother, wife, children, lands…a cross! It may mean persecution from your own home; it may mean breaking your heart. It may mean going out as the off-scourings of the world and being regarded as a fool! "Take up thy cross, and follow me!"

And where is He going? Well, He proceeds to tell the disciples. He is going up to Jerusalem: "Behold, we go up to Jerusalem; and the Son of man shall be delivered unto the chief priests, and unto the scribes; and they shall condemn him to death, and they shall deliver him to the Gentiles: And they shall mock him, and shall scourge him, and shall spit upon him, and shall kill him…" (Mk 10:33–34). Christianity is something marvellous and wonderful, and the whole world will praise you? No! A cross, a shame, to be despised, to be reviled, to be a fool for Christ's sake: that is what He calls you to. Not world reform, not popularity, not rejoicing, but the exact opposite. "This is the way," He says. And it is because He said things like that to him that this young man went away sorrowful.

So, he went away because of what Christ did not say and he went away, too, because of what Christ did say.

Then, thirdly, he went away sorrowful because he went away from Christ. He did not realise his real need. He thought he was all right though he needed something extra, but he did not understand that he was lost, that he was under the wrath of God. He did not realise he was helpless and hopeless, that he was outside the kingdom and that if he remained there he would go to Hell. He was not desperate.

That is the trouble of these people who go away from Christ. They come in intellectual interest, they come to put very good questions, they are good people as far as they go. But in a sense that is their trouble, they have never realised that they are lost, that they are sinners, and that they cannot save themselves. They have never understood what is awaiting them, that their position is desperate and hopeless. If the young man had only realised that, he would never have gone away. He would have stayed and clung to Him as the only possible hope: but he had never seen that.

Furthermore, he did not realise who Christ was, and why He had come into the world. He had regarded Him as just a very good man and an exceptional teacher; the unique teacher, the greatest teacher, perhaps, that had ever appeared; but He was nothing more. So Christ pulled him up. When he said, "Good Master, what shall I do that I may inherit eternal life?", Jesus said to him, "Why callest thou me good?" "Do you realise," He said in effect, "what you are saying? Listen to the word you have used yourself; you have said I am 'good', and you are right. There is only one who is good, that is God, and you have applied it to me. But you do not know what you are saying. You are, incidently, speaking the truth—I am the Son of God! I am one who has come out of eternity into time. I am God the Son come down on earth."

The young man did not realise it, but this is the truth. He put the right question: "What shall I do that I may inherit eternal life?" And what our Lord was really telling him is this: "I am eternal life! You have put your question to the right person. 'I am come that they might have life, and that they might have it more abundantly' (Jn 10:10)—and I am able to do that because I am who I am. A man cannot give you eternal life, but I can because I have come to do it. I am the giver of life; I am life itself. I am come from God, and He sent me 'to seek and to save that which is lost'. Look at me, realise what you are saying, I am the answer to all your questions. I am the light of the world, I am the life of the world, I am everything, it is all in me."

But the young man did not realise this. If he had only realised his need and his lost estate and his condition and that this was the Son of God who was sent to save the world—"the Lamb of God which taketh away the sin of the world" (Jn 1:29)—he would never have left Him, he would have said, "I believe; take me in." He had not realised the truth about himself, or about the Son of God, the Saviour of his soul.

And, lastly, he had completely failed to realise the truth about the treasure in heaven. "One thing thou lackest: go thy way, sell whatsoever thou hast, and give to the poor, and thou shalt have treasure in heaven." He was an expert on the treasure he had on earth, but ignorant of the heavenly treasure. He did not know anything about the joy of forgiveness; he did not know what it is to be given new life, to become a child and a son of God.

Poor man, he had got his estate. It was wonderful, the biggest estate in the district and the envy of all the other landowners. "But my dear man," said Christ, "if you put that by the side of the other inheritance that may be yours if you believe in me, it is nothing." Heirship of heaven and of God; joint-heirship with Christ and the glory of eternity that awaits the children of God—he knew nothing about it. He was so keen on time that he ignored eternity. All he had got would soon be gone, and when he died he would have to leave it behind him because he could not take it with him. All his estate, his wealth, his property, his everything, was there, crumbling and decaying, and he would die: "Naked came I out of my mother's womb, and naked shall I return thither," said Job. Empty handed!

"Lay not up for yourselves treasure upon earth," says Christ, "where moth and rust doth corrupt, and thieves break through and steal: but lay up for yourselves treasure in heaven, where neither moth nor rust doth corrupt, and where thieves do not break through nor steal" (Mt 6:19–20). *There* is the place to put your treasure! But this young man know nothing about it, he was so interested in the present that he did not consider the future. That is why he went away sorrowful; he went away from Christ!

These, then, are the lessons taught us by this rich young ruler. Have you learned them? Have you realised the danger of relying on anything in yourself—money, intellect, morality, good living, good behaviour, philanthropy—put in anything you like? If you are relying on any of them, you are outside the kingdom. That is the first lesson: the fatal error of relying on anything, putting your trust in anything that you have or that you can do.

The second lesson is that to turn away from Christ always leads to sorrow. You will never have happiness in this world apart from Christ. You may think you have, but it will not last. It is a world of sin and shame, a world of unhappiness, and of disappointments. Sorrow is the lot of all who turn their backs on Christ. Judas later turned his back upon Him—he went out, "and it was night" (Jn 13:30), and he committed suicide. To leave Christ is always a spiritual suicide. You are turning away from your Saviour, away from life which is life indeed, away from the Son of God who came to die for you and to save you; you are turning from the only one who can give you happiness, peace and joy. "Thou hast made us for thyself, and our hearts are restless until they find their rest in thee," said Augustine. There is no resting-place in life in this world apart from Christ, and if you leave Him, you are always going to sorrow.

It is like that in this world, but what of the next! To turn your back on Christ in this life means eternal misery in the next. That is the lesson of the ten virgins, the five foolish ones who came when it was too late and hammered at the door. "Open unto us!" they cried. "No! Too late!" was the reply. And they remained in their folly and in their misery.

Consider too, the story of the rich man and Lazarus in Luke 16. He again saw it too late. He wanted a message sent to his brethren lest they should do the same thing and be guilty of the same folly. "Go and tell them," he said…but it was too late! Eternal misery! "God so loved the world, that he gave his only begotten Son, that whosoever believeth in him should not perish" (Jn 3:16)—but if they do not, they perish, and perish everlastingly! To turn your back on Christ is always to go away sorrowful. It leads to sorrow, and it ends there. God grant that we learn the lesson of this rich young ruler about the way of entry into the kingdom of God. One of our hymns puts it like this:

> Jesus call us! O'er the tumult
>   Of our life's wild restless sea,
> Day by day His sweet voice soundeth,
>   Saying, "Christian, follow me":
>
> Jesus calls us from the worship
>   Of the vain world's golden store,
> From each idol that would keep us,
>   Saying, "Christian, love me more!"

Have you heard Him? Have you heard His voice calling you? This Son of God who can give you eternal life and everlasting bliss and joy—He is calling you. Can you say with the hymnwriter,

> Jesus calls us! By Thy mercies,
>   Saviour, may we hear Thy call,
> Give our hearts to Thy obedience,
>   Serve and love Thee best of all.
>   Cecil Frances Alexander

Oh do not go away from Him! If you leave Him you have left your last and only hope; there is nothing remaining but grief and everlasting unhappiness. Do not go away from Him, but, just as you are, give yourself to Him. Let Him speak to you, as He has spoken to you. He has exposed your real trouble, your real sin, the thing you are holding on to instead of Him.

Consider who He is, consider what He can do for you, consider the joy that remains for you, if you "sell all that you have" as it were, and take up your cross and go after Him. Hear Him I plead with you, do not turn your back on Him, or you will go to endless misery. Fall at His feet, look up into His face and say to Him, "Here I am; take me."

> Just as I am, without one plea
> But that Thy blood was shed for me,
> And that Thou bidd'st me come to Thee,
>   O Lamb of God, I come.
> Charlotte Elliott

If you have never said that to Him before say it now before it is too late.

10 SO NEAR AND YET SO FAR

One of the scribes came, and having heard them [our Lord and the Herodians and Sadducees] reasoning together, and perceiving that he had answered them well, asked him, Which is the first commandment of all? And Jesus answered him, The first of all the commandments is, Hear O Israel; The Lord our God is one Lord: And thou shalt love the Lord thy God with all thy heart, and with all thy soul, and with all thy mind, and with all thy strength: this is the first commandment. And the second is like, namely, this, Thou shalt love thy neighbour as thyself. There is none other commandment greater than these. And the scribe said unto him, Well, Master, thou hast said the truth: for there is one God; and there is none other but he: And to love him with all the heart, and with all the understanding, and with all the soul, and with all the strength, and to love his neighbour as himself, is more than all whole burnt offerings and sacrifices. And when Jesus saw that he answered discreetly, he said unto him, Thou art not far from the kingdom of God. And no man after that durst ask him any question (Mk 12:28–34).

WE FIND IN THESE VERSES yet another cause of misunderstanding about the kingdom of God; another man who is in difficulties about it all. But in coming to this man we come to one who has certain features which entitle us to say that he is in an advanced position with respect to all the others. Here is a man who won an encomium from our Lord, even a word of encouragement. Here is the first case we have considered where our Lord has said, "Thou art not far from the kingdom." So here we are moving forward a little. Here is a man who can be described, if you like, as "on the way". There are some who have not moved and are far away; but not this man. He is almost in the kingdom.

So this scribe obviously has certain features which put him in a category on his own. He is not like those whom we have been considering—the men at the end of Luke 9 or the rich young ruler. Nor, indeed, is he like the members of the church at Corinth, who seemed to think that it was enough to say, "Lord, Lord!" and were not very careful about their lives. They were deceiving themselves and had to be told that "the unrighteous shall not inherit the kingdom of God."

No, this man represents an advance; and as we come to analyse his case, I think we shall see that he represents large numbers of people at the present time. What an odd position this is! But the matter divides itself up, it seems to me, quite naturally and inevitably in terms of what our Lord said about the man. "When Jesus saw that he answered discreetly, he said unto him, Thou art not far from the kingdom of God."

There are, then, three great principles here. The first is a general point about our relationship to the kingdom. There is the kingdom, and our Lord says about this scribe, "Thou art not far from the kingdom"; he is in relationship to it. But this statement of our Lord's throws very great light upon this question, and there are many who go wrong at this point so let me expound this in a little more detail.

The first thing that stands out here very clearly, as of course it does in the whole of the New Testament, is—let me emphasise this again—that there is no vagueness nor any indefiniteness about our relationship to the kingdom of God. We are either in it or outside it. But the whole tragedy of today is that people think that this is a very vague matter. We are living in an age, as we have already seen, that dislikes doctrine, or definitions, or theology. Christianity, we are told, is a vague general spirit, something that you "catch": "Christianity is caught not taught" and so on. You cannot say that a man is a Christian, or that he is not a Christian; the only position is that everybody can hope that they are Christians, but you cannot define these things.

But that is a blank contradiction of the plain teaching of the Scriptures. "Thou art not far from the kingdom." In other words, you are not in it, you are outside it. Our Lord can tell whether a man is in or out. The teaching everywhere in the Bible is that people themselves should be able to tell what their position is. You see, this is not a question of some kind of oasis in the midst of a surrounding country. Not at all! The kingdom of God is sharply defined and there is a gate of entry into it. We go further; our Lord says it is a "strait gate". It is not a very broad and wide one where people can slip in, and you are not sure whether they have gone in or not, or who has gone in, or how many have gone in. No! It is a narrow gate, which leads to "a narrow way". Indeed we can put it like this: the strait gate of entry into the kingdom is a turnstile, and it only admits one at a time.

You may say, "But you can have a large number of converts in a meeting." All right! But in the sight of God, they are individuals. You cannot go in crowds into the kingdom. God deals with us one by one. This is an individual matter. We cannot be saved in families. The fact that your parents were Christians does not mean that you are a Christian. The fact that your forbears have always been Christians does not mean that you are one. Nor is there any such thing as "a Christian country". No, this is a very individual matter; we come face to face with God one by one, and God looks upon us and deals with us in that way. There is a time in the life of every one who is a citizen of the kingdom of God when, like Jacob of old, you are left alone; when you are isolated from your nearest and dearest, and you are alone face to face with God. It is an individual matter.

This is obviously a very vital point. If people are not sure whether they are Christians or not, then I take leave to suggest that they are not. The Christian, according to the New Testament, is someone who can say something like this: "I was—I am." That was how the Apostle described the Corinthians, was it not? He said, "And such were some of you!" They had been drunkards, adulterers, fornicators, etc. "But," he says, "you are not like that now—'Ye are washed, but ye are sanctified, but ye are justified in the name of the Lord Jesus, and by the Spirit of our God'." The Apostle Peter used exactly the same terminology: "Which in time past were not a people, but are now the people of God: which had not obtained mercy, but now have obtained mercy" (1 Pet 2:10). That is it!

The Apostle Paul, again, says to the Colossians, "Who hath delivered us from the power of darkness, and hath translated us into the kingdom of his dear Son" (Col 1:13). There is a movement, something has happened. And he knows that it has happened to them and they themselves know that it has happened as well. You cannot receive the life of God in your soul and be doubtful as to whether anything has happened to you. No, this thing is quite clear. Men and women are either in the kingdom or else they are outside it. You "who sometimes were far off are made nigh by the blood of Christ," writes the Apostle Paul to the Ephesians (Eph 2:13). So all this modern suggestion that there is indefiniteness about this is of the devil.

But secondly, under this heading, though there is no vagueness, we are nevertheless entitled to say that there are variations in people's relative positions with respect to this kingdom. Our Lord said about this man, "Thou *art not far from* the kingdom." He did not say that about everybody, but He did say it about him. So outside the kingdom people can be in one of many, many positions.

We have seen what the Apostle wrote to the members of the Ephesian church. They were Gentiles, and the Gentiles he describes are people who were "far off". but he does not describe the Jews, before they became Christians, in that way. They were "near". They were in a very different position from the pagans; they were on the very doorstep of the kingdom, while the others were about as far away from the kingdom as anyone can possibly be. The Gentiles were polytheists. Look at the people in Athens—the whole place was cluttered up with their temples to their various gods. But the Jews had advanced well beyond that, they knew that there was only one God, and so they were much nearer than those who were still in paganism.

And it is still true to say that there are men and women who are in very different positions with respect to their relationship to the kingdom of God. There are people who have never given it a thought; who have never read the Bible and are not interested in it, they do not know its barest elements. They are not interested in God, in the Lord Jesus Christ or in the soul and they live the kind of life that we can see all around us.

But there are others who are very interested in these things. They read their Bibles, attend services, listen to lectures on the radio and read books about Christianity; they are concerned. They are not in the same position as the others. "Thou art not far from..." Our Lord did not say that about anybody else. This is the first time we have come across that in our consideration of where people stand in relation to the kingdom of God.

And then, thirdly, is it not amazing to notice how far one can travel in the direction of the kingdom of God and yet still be outside it? Here this man is standing, as it were, just outside that gate, but he is still outside. Now, as we read the gospels, we see that our Lord seems to be the complete antithesis of many a modern evangelist. Far from doing everything He can to drag people in, he seems to be keeping them out. We have already had illustrations of that. He seems to make it difficult. There is great truth in that, as we shall see. But we cannot but be struck by the fact that a man can come so far and still not be in.

And that leads me to my final point under this first general principle, which is that though there are these different and varying positions occupied by men and women outside the kingdom of God, in the last analysis they do not matter at all. There is no advantage in being "not far from the kingdom". "But," you say, "do you mean to say that the person who is at the very door has no advantage over the one who is, as it were, at the other end of the world?" Precisely! And that is where the devil deludes so many.

That, it seems to me, was the essential trouble with this man. This is where we fool ourselves. We say, "Look at that man there living in vice and sin, never giving God a thought, there he is far far away from the kingdom. But *I* am not there; I am very interested, I am standing just outside the door." But what advantage is it to you, when the end comes, that you are just outside the door? That does not mean that you are in. You are no more in the kingdom than that man who is so far away— "So near, and yet so far!" On the very threshold; but what does it matter, how does it help? We recognise these differences, but finally they are of no value; they will be of no avail at the bar of eternal judgment.

Let me use a simple and an obvious illustration. You may be standing in a bus queue, you have had a very heavy day and you are tired. And suddenly the bus comes along and you begin to feel hopeful and happy; you say, "Now I shall soon be on my way home." The queue is moving forward and so are you, and the person right in front of you has just got on. Suddenly the conductor holds out his hand and you are not allowed on. You were almost in, but the trouble is you were not in, and you have to wait until the next bus comes. The fact that you were the next one to get on does not mean that you *have* got on. The bus has gone without you and you are left standing in the queue.

It is exactly like that here: "Thou art not far from the kingdom." Oh how easily it can be misunderstood! The Lord was praising the man, there is no question about that, but what is the value of it—the man is outside, not in. And therefore I ask this one question as I finish this section: Do you know that you are in the kingdom of God?

That, then, was our first principle—the general one about

our relationship to the kingdom. The second point is this: Why did our Lord say about this man—and this applies to all who are like him—that he was "not far from the kingdom of God"? This is praise; our Lord obviously liked him and He liked certain things about him, so He said in effect, "You are not far from the kingdom: I will say that about you." What is it that brings a person into this position? And here, they key word is the word *discreetly*. We are told in verse 34 that "Jesus saw that he answered discreetly." That is quite a good translation but let me give you some others which will help to bring out the meaning. "When Jesus saw that he answered intelligently"; or "when Jesus saw that he answered sensibly." Those are equally good renderings of the word.

Now this is a very interesting point for us. Whatever we have to say against this man, our Lord tells us that he had an intelligent interest in the kingdom of God. I emphasise this, of course, because the average person today thinks that the only people who are Christians are the unintelligent! Modern man, come of age! The scientific era! And anybody who is still a Christian is just an ignoramus. Sob-stuff! Emotionalism! Is not that the common idea? People dismiss Christianity, though they know nothing at all about it. And there is only one thing to say about such people—they are completely unintelligent! Our Lord praises this man for being intelligent, and for using his mind and his reason.

Let me put this very plainly. There is nothing that I know of under heaven that makes me think so much as this Gospel! On many a Sunday there are those who have spent their day reading the Sunday newspapers with the gossip and all the rest of it. But they are too intelligent to come to a place of worship! They are too intelligent to be Christians. But it is the exact opposite, you see. There is nothing that so makes men and women reason and ponder and meditate as this blessed Gospel of the glorious God; and when our Lord finds a man thinking and using the faculties that God has given him, He says "Good!" He saw that he had answered intelligently, "discreetly".

How, then, did the man use his intelligence? First of all,

because he was using his mind and his reason, he was not antagonistic to our Lord and he did not come to Him just in order to trip Him and to catch Him. We are told that certain Pharisees and Herodians were sent to "catch Him in His words" (Mk 12:13); and they came praising our Lord and fawning; but He saw through all: "He, knowing their hypocrisy, said unto them, Why tempt ye me?..." (v 15).

But this scribe did not come to our Lord just to put a trick question in order to get Him into confusion, and in order that he could take Him up on a word and then have the pleasure of having caught Him. The Pharisees, the Herodians and the Sadducees did not want knowledge, or information; they did not want help. They were just out to be clever. But this man is too intelligent for that; it is only unintelligent people who do that sort of thing.

And you, are you still in the stage of saying that you are not a Christian because you do not know who Cain's wife was? Or are you still saying, "I am not a Christian because...what about that fish that swallowed Jonah?" Are you still bringing out the old chestnuts? If you are, you are just showing that you are not intelligent; that is just being childish. As if you could dismiss the whole of the Bible and the whole story of the Christian Church and of Christianity by just being clever and bringing out your trick questions!

But I am assuming that you are like this man; that you have sense; that you have a certain amount of understanding, and that you are not out just to down Christianity. I take it that you are so much a failure in life yourself, and that you are so amazed at the world today that you say, "This is no time for playing or for being clever. We want truth, we want a knowledge of God and we want to know if this Gospel will help us!"

But secondly, the man demonstrated that he was intelligent by showing that he had an appreciation of our Lord Himself. We read here, "One of the scribes came, and having heard them reasoning together, and perceiving that he had answered them well, asked him..." (Mk 12:28). You see, he was not a Christian, nor a believer in the Lord Jesus Christ, but he had been listening to this disputation between our Lord and the others and he said to himself, "This is a remarkable person. He is only a carpenter but he has wonderful insight." He liked the way our Lord answered; He noticed that He had handled them well and that He had answered them well, and he was man enough, and honest and intelligent enough to say, "This person is someone I want to question, this man can tell me something." He was drawn by Jesus and His personality and this is a very good thing to say about a man.

Have you come face to face with the person of Jesus of Nazareth? Have you felt that there is someone here with whom you must reckon; that there has been a personality in this world that stands out above everyone else? And are you ready to listen to Him?

Furthermore this scribe had shown appreciation of our Lord's teaching also, and of His answers; he noticed that "he had answered them well". Our Lord in answering the other people had shown a very profound understanding of the Scriptures, and this man was a scribe. It was his business to copy the Scriptures. He said, "This man knows His Scriptures, and I like His interpretation of them. In answering these others, He does not philosophize but quotes Scriptures to them." And this man liked that, because he knew that ultimately we have no knowledge in these matters at all apart from what we have in the Scriptures. Christianity is not a philosophy, it is not what men conjure up in their own minds. We know nothing apart from what has been revealed, and here is one who stands on the Revelation; and the scribe liked Him for that and appreciated it.

And not only that; he noticed how, in dealing with the Sadducees, our Lord had not only asserted and defended, He had preached the doctrine of the Resurrection. The Sadducees did not believe in it and He had given them a quotation of Scripture that immediately put them into difficulties. He believed in the resurrection, and this man appreciated that, because, as a scribe, he believed in it. There was a division on this between these people and the Sadducees. So he had an appreciation of Christian teaching and of Christian doctrine and he noticed, too, our Lord's emphasis upon the soul. "Render...unto Caesar," He had said, "the things that are Caesar's; but unto God the things that are God's" (Mt 22:21). He liked this emphasis upon the soul, upon the coming judgment and the Resurrection—"All that," he said, "is sound teaching and doctrine."

But he went further. Notice how he added something to what our Lord said to him. He asked his question—"Which is the first and the greatest commandment of all?" Our Lord gave the answer: "Thou shalt love the Lord thy God with all thy heart, and with all thy soul, and with all thy mind, and with all thy strength: This is the first commandment. The second is like unto it, Thou shalt love thy neighbour as thyself." Then, "the scribe said unto him, Well, Master, Thou hast said the truth: for there is one God."

That was absolutely vital to him. This was the peculiar treasure that had been given to the Jews, this belief in the knowledge of the one and only true and living God—"and there is none other." "And," he added, "to love him with all the understanding, and with all the soul, and with all the strength, and to love his neighbour as himself, is more than all whole burnt offerings and sacrifices."

Now our Lord had not mentioned that, but this man was intelligent and he showed here very clearly that it is no use relying upon forms of religion, "burnt offerings and sacrifices". That was what so many people were doing. They believed in God, but they went on sinning. They said, "I have sinned against God but if I take a burnt offering it will be all right. If I do something terrible it does not matter, because I will take a sacrifice." It is the attitude which says, "Live as you like, then go and confess to the priest and all will be cleared! Get down on your knees; do some good acts, give a donation to some good cause; the good you do cancels out the evil you do"—"Burnt offerings and sacrifices!"

It is this dependence upon externals in religion; upon good deeds as a way of pleasing God. It is this foolish, unintelligent belief that God can be bought; that as long as we pay an occasional visit to His house everything is cleared; as long as we now and again go out of our way and offer something to Him by way of a sacrifice, God is going to give the "All clear" to us and we are going to be happy ever afterwards. No, said this man, God cannot be bought in that way.

And then he went on to the next point. He realised the essential demand of God's Law, and the essentially spiritual character of that demand. "These others," he said in effect, "are arguing about the details and the minutiae of the Law, they 'tithe mint and rue and anise and cummin'. It is all wrong, they have never seen the spiritual character of the Law. Being right with God is not just a collection of mechanics or of isolated details. The thing that God calls for is that man should love Him with the whole of his being and serve Him, and love his neighbour as himself." He had a spiritual understanding of the Law, and that is a tremendous thing to say about someone.

The Pharisees, in general, had not got it. They said that as long as they did not actually murder a man physically, then the commandment which says, "Thou shalt not kill," was all right as far as they were concerned. They said, "I have never actually committed adultery, therefore I can smile in the face of the commandment which says 'Thou shalt not commit adultery'." But our Lord interprets those commandments like this: "Whosoever shall say to his brother, Thou fool, shall be in danger of hell fire" (Mt 5:22)—you have already murdered him. And, "Whosoever looketh on a woman to lust after her has committed adultery with her already in his heart." It is the spiritual nature of the Law.

But, above all, God demands a total allegiance to Himself; God wants men and women to live to Him and to His glory; He has made them for that and He expects that from them. This man had seen all that, and because of that, our Lord said to him, "Thou art not far from the kingdom of God."

You see how he had advanced, you see the steps he had taken, you see his interest, his concern? He was on the very threshold, so our Lord said to him in effect, "You have seen that God is calling upon men to live to His glory. He wants their love, it is His totalitarian demand. You have seen through the uselessness of all sham and pretence and works and externals in religion, you have seen the spiritual character of it all. You have seen it, and you are not far from the kingdom."

And yet he was still outside the kingdom. He was not far from it, he was looking in through the door, through the gate, as it were, but that was no good, he was not inside. So why was that excellent scribe still only in that position? Well, the answer does not need any critical or exegetical acumen in order to explain it, it is all here on the surface.

The first reason is that his interest was only theoretical and intellectual, and that is where he comes as such a warning to many good intelligent young people at the present time, and, indeed, to middle-aged and older people also. There he was, he had been listening to our Lord arguing and debating with the Pharisees and Herodians, and then with the Sadducees. He said, "This is wonderful; I have never known anybody like this man. He has a command; He has understanding and insight; He marshals His Scriptures, and He is wonderful in His argumentation. So let us hear what He has to say about this. His opinion is rather worth having." And so he puts his question.

Now religion can be very interesting, and it is still fairly popular. Controversial books published on the subject can become best sellers because it is always a good talking point. People say, "You know, I am very interested in religion. I never go to a place of worship of course, but I like reading about it and talking about it, and arguing and debating about it." And they do, and in a sense they are perfectly genuine. But it is all just intellectual—"Which is the first and the greatest commandment?"—"I am interested in that," said the scribe in effect, "I know the arguments and I know the arguments of my fellow-scribes and Pharisees. I am well aware of all that, but you know it seems to me to be beside the point. Now I would like to know which *you* think is the first and the greatest, I should be so interested to know your answer."

I have met dozens of people who are in that position. They are very nice people, generally intellectual and they say that they are "very intrigued about this whole matter of religion" and they are anxious to have my opinion on this, that and the other. But it never goes further than that, it stops at the level of the intellect, it is something purely theoretical. This is a terrible thing; let us warn one another and let us all warn everybody about this. Men and women may think that they are Christians but what they are really interested in is theology.

Now there is nothing more intelligent than to be interested in theology. Some of the greatest books ever written have been about this. You grapple with these philosophical problems and that is why these books sell. What is God? Is He up there, or is He out there...and so on. "Ah, this is wonderful," people say. "I do like reading books which tell me something about the being of God.." And so, God becomes a subject, and we investigate it and look into it. But the terrible thing is that so many stop at that point. This man stopped there and I can prove that because, secondly, with all his interest in the Law and the first and the chiefest point of the Law, it never seemed to occur to him that he ought to ask the question: "Have I kept the Law?" Is this not almost inconceivable? Here is a man who in response to our Lord, says, in effect, "Well done, Jesus, you have given a marvellous answer! I am in entire agreement with what you say." And he leaves it at that.

That is the tragedy. The first and the chiefest commandment of God is that I should love Him with all my heart and soul and mind and strength, and my neighbour as myself; but the moment I agree with that then surely I ought to go on and ask this question: Am I doing that? If this is what God asks me to do then have I done it? But the man is content purely with an intellectual answer, and he does not go any further. "Quite right," he says; "you know that is what I always say in the arguments myself. We have had many of these discussions and I have always said that this is the first and the chiefest thing. You are quite right, Master..."

But the Law of God is not here for you to applaud, it is here for you to apply. Paul puts it like this: "Not the hearers of the law are just before God, but the doers of the law shall be justified" (Rom 2:13). And this is where this man fails, and fails so lamentably. It was the trouble with the whole nation of the Jews. They said, "We are God's people. God has given us the Law; but those Gentiles are without the pale, they have not got a law, they are law-less people." And they thought that because they had the Law, all was well and they were saved.

No, says Paul, the fact that you have got it does not mean that you are right; have you kept it? God has not made you just custodians and guardians of the Law. He does not want you to agree with it, He wants you to practise it. And this foolish man never faced the question.

But have you settled the question? The Law demands that you carry it out, that you fulfil it. Have you done so? It is because this scribe never faced it that he was not in the kingdom; he was still outside. He had an intelligent understanding and he agreed, but he had not applied it, he stopped when he should have gone on. He should have said, "Well, in the light of that..." But he had never repented.

But let me show you something still more important. He did not go on to ask the question that follows that, which is: what does a man do when he realises that he has not kept the Law? He did not say, 'There is the law of God, I will have to face it at the bar of eternal judgment. I have not kept it, so what do I do?' This man was so pleased that our Lord agreed with what he had always said, and that he had got the answer he expected that he was ready to go away; everything was all right. There was no acknowledgement of failure, no sense of need. He did not realise his need of salvation, he was a pure theorist, just interested in religion. He did not see that what he agreed with condemned him and put him in this precarious position where he should be desperate. He did not ask this vital question: "What must I do to be saved?"

And that brings me to my very last point which is that he never realised who the Lord Jesus Christ was and why He had come into this world, because if he had, he would not have left off at that point. If he had seen the real significance of what the Law is and his own failure to keep it; it he had seen that therefore he was under the wrath of God and excluded from the life of God, he would have realised his need. He would have cried for help, and especially he would have asked this Person who was standing before him, whom he admired so much, who had got such a grasp of the Scriptures, and who seemed to have such insight and understanding, he would have turned to Him and fallen on his knees and said, "Can you help me, I have not kept the law, I have broken it, I do not love God, no man can. Can you help me?" But he did not come near to asking that question.

He did not realise, above all, that the only one who can help a person in that position was the very one to whom he gave his original question. For if he had but realised that He was the Son of God incarnate, the everlasting Word made flesh, walking the roads of Galilee, teaching, working miracles, soon to be nailed on a Cross; if he had understood that, then he would have realised that this Son of God had come into the world for this very reason—because the whole world is indeed guilty before God. He came into the world because the Law of God condemns us all. No one has loved God, no one can in the sense demanded; nor his neighbour as himself. We are therefore all lost, but "the Son of man has come to seek and to save that which is lost!" Paul writes to the Galatians, "He was made of a woman, made under the law"—what for?—"to redeem them that are under the law" (Gal 4:4–5). We cannot get into the kingdom of God unless we keep this Law, and we cannot. There is only one who ever kept it and He came into the world in order to do so. He became a man in order that He might put himself under this Law that condemns us, and He lived it, He honoured it, He kept it to the full, He did not fail in any iota.

But He went even beyond that. The Law of God had to be honoured and He honoured it. But the Law had been broken and the punishment for the breaking of the Law is death: "The wages of sin is death" (Rom 6:23). Here is the condemnation of the Law upon sin and evil and transgression, and it will exact its penalty. So he came and took on Him human nature, and lived and went to the Cross to receive the penalty of the broken Law of God. "The Lord hath laid on him the iniquity of us all" (Is 53:6). He has borne my punishment: the Law is satisfied positively and negatively. The Law is answered and God offers me a free forgiveness.

This man, finally, was not far from the kingdom, but he was still outside it, because he had not realised that the only way to enter it was to believe on the name of the only begotten Son of God. He had not understood that the only way to enter the kingdom is to have "repentance toward God, and faith toward our Lord Jesus Christ" (Acts 20:21). He had not been broken and seen his helplessness and hopelessness, and he had not turned to this blessed Son of God and said, "Have mercy upon me! Look down upon me, redeem me, save me, I trust my all to you."

God deliver us from a mere intellectual, theoretical interest in religion and in the kingdom of God! Have you heard the Law of God speaking to you? The question that every one of us will have to answer at the eternal bar of judgment is, Have you loved the Lord your God with all your heart, and all your soul, and all your mind, and all your strength; and your neighbour as yourself? It will be no use telling God of all the good you have done; that is not what He asks of you. He wants your heart, He wants your life, He wants you!

There is only one way to be right with God, it is to fall with adoration and simple belief at the feet of the one who said, "I am come that they might have life, and that they might have it more abundantly" (Jn 10:10). "Christ is the end of the law for righteousness to everyone that believeth" said Paul (Rom 10:4). Have you believed? If you have, you are in the kingdom. If you have not, however near you may be, you are on the outside, and if you die like that you will remain in everlasting misery. Believe on the Lord Jesus Christ and be saved.

11 BORN AGAIN

Jesus answered and said unto him, Verily, verily, I say unto thee, Except a man be born again, he cannot see the kingdom of God. Jesus answered, Verily, verily I say unto thee, Except a man be born of water and of the Spirit, he cannot enter into the kingdom of God (Jn 3:3,5).

THE GREATEST NEED OF THE HUMAN RACE, as we have seen, is to come back to the kingdom of God, to the reign and rule of God and to the blessing of God. And yet, the whole time we have found this crass misunderstanding about the very beginnings, the elements, the fundamentals of the Christian faith and of the teaching concerning the kingdom of God. And so our Lord had to spend so much of His time in this world, the short, precious three years, in argumentation and disputation, answering questions and so on. Yet He did so very readily, because He had come to help people, he had come to enlighten them and to show them the way. And so with great patience He listened to their questions and He answered them.

Now here we come to another misunderstanding of the kingdom as it is depicted in this well-known story of our Lord's interview with Nicodemus. It is one of the great stories of the whole of Scripture, it is such a dramatic story. This master of Israel, a Pharisee, a teacher, seeking an interview late at night with this—*carpenter*? Not an official teacher at all, but, nevertheless, a man who had been preaching and teaching and working miracles. What a wonderful encounter it was! If you are merely interested in drama, this story is worth considering.

But, even more, what wonderful truth comes out here! That is what we are concerned about, because I would suggest that our Lord puts the whole thing much more plainly here than He did perhaps anywhere else. In nearly all the other cases we have been dealing with, He was dealing with particular difficulties and answering questions. He does not do that here. In this story of Nicodemus, He puts it as clearly and as distinctly as He ever did.

We are coming to the end of this series; we have been following it in steps and stages, and we have seen people, as it were, coming nearer and nearer. The man in our last study was not far from the kingdom. And now, in these verses, and in Matthew 18:1– 4, we find the two clearest statements on this matter in the whole of the New Testament. In Matthew we read, "At the same time came the disciples unto Jesus, saying, Who is the greatest in the kingdom of heaven? And Jesus called a little child unto him, and set him in the midst of them, And said, Verily I say unto you, Except ye be converted and become as little children, ye shall not enter into the kingdom of heaven"—words which say exactly the same thing as these verses in John.

Now here we come to the very heart of the matter, to the real secret of this business of entering the kingdom of God. We have looked at our Lord's words: "Seek ye first the kingdom of God and his righteousness, and all these things shall be added unto you." But how can I do so? How can I enter? And here, our Lord really gives us a plain and final answer to this vital question, and He does so in a most interesting manner. He does so not only by what He says to Nicodemus, but also in the way in which He handles him.

Here we have a very remarkable thing; unlike the scribe in our last study, Nicodemus is not even allowed to ask his question. Notice this: "There was a man of the Pharisees, named Nicodemus, a ruler of the Jews: The same came to Jesus by night and said unto Him, Rabbi, we know that thou art a teacher come from God: for no man can do these miracles that thou doest, except God be with him..." Suddenly he is interrupted. "Jesus answered and said unto him, Verily, verily, I say unto thee, Except a man be born again, he cannot see the kingdom of God." Nicodemus has asked nothing, he has simply praised our Lord, and our Lord interrupts him. He is going on to put a question, but he is not allowed to do so.

And our Lord, by interrupting him immediately, as I want to show you, is teaching us a very great lesson, and bringing out the profound truth about the nature of His kingdom and about the only way whereby it can be entered. He interrupts him like that in order that He might suddenly pull him up, arrest him and apprehend him and show him the whole thing in a nutshell.

Let me first comment on this extraordinary behaviour of our Lord in two respects before I come to my analysis. The first thing, of course, that strikes one about this incident is our Lord's own person. What knowledge He has, what understanding He possesses. John 2:23–25 tells us, let me remind you again, "Jesus did not commit himself unto them, because he knew all men, and needed not that any should testify of man: for he knew what was in man." And here is a perfect illustration of that. Here comes this Pharisee, this "ruler of the Jews", this "master of Israel", this man who is in the privileged position of being an instructor of the common people in religion and in the Law of God, and our Lord interrupts him! He can read his mind, He knows him, He sees through him, because Nicodemus is there before Him as an open book.

This is one of the proofs of the fact that He is the Son of God. He knows what Nicodemus is going to say. He knows the type, He knows this particular man. He knows that Nicodemus, after this preliminary salutation, is going to say, "Master, what I want is this: I want to know what this good thing is that you have got. I am a master in Israel; I am a teacher; what is this something extra you have? I know all the other teachers and I have admired them, but, you know, you are in a class above us. What is it? I want it. What must I do?" But he is not allowed to say it.

Here, then, we have this wonderful manifestation of His Godhead, His unique divinity. Here He is as man amongst men, and apparently but a common man, a carpenter, but what insight! And when you come near to Him, if you read your Bible with open eyes and meet Him in the New Testament, He will examine you; He will search you, and tell you all about yourself, and you will know it. That is what we call "conviction of sin". He reads us as open books. We cannot conceal anything from Him. He tears away all the camouflage and the sham, and all our intellectuality and sophistication become as tawdry nothing when it is face to face with this penetrating gaze of the only begotten Son of God.

And the second comment is that Nicodemus proves that our Lord's knowledge of him is absolutely right. He does that, as we shall see, by the stupid things he says and by the foolish questions that he asks. Our Lord has not got time to waste on this occasion. He has been preaching, he has worked His miracles, and He is tired. Not only that, He wants to bring this man to a right position, so He stops him, indeed, He is almost violent with him. Why? Well, here is a great man and he must be handled as such, and our Lord shows him exactly where he goes wrong. That is the purpose of this sudden and unusual interruption. It is almost unique in the stories that we are told of our Lord in the New Testament.

So by doing that, and then by saying what He does, our Lord gives us here this plain, clear, unequivocal teaching about the kingdom of God and about the only way to enter into it. It is a great crucial statement which none can afford to ignore. Here is the real answer to the modern confusion, because the modern attitude is this, is it not? If we are to get the Gospel over to modern, scientific men and women, then, as we have seen, we are told that we must abandon all this terminology of the Bible, and we must sit with them and drink with them and curse with them and do many other things with them. We meet them on their own level and then they will begin to get it.

But here is the answer to all that. You see, modern men and women need to be interrupted. They are clever, they think they are clever, they think they know yet they obviously do not know how to live, do they; but they think they do; they think they know everything. Yet what they need is not to be wheedled or flattered, but to be interrupted, to be silenced. And I believe that that is what God is doing. This is the greatest need of the world today. It needs to be interrupted, in all its clever folly, by the Word of the living God.

Now our Lord makes three propositions here. The first is simply a repetition of His own words: "Ye must be born again." He throws down the gauntlet. He says, in effect, "It is all right; I know what you are going to say, but you need not say it, it is all wrong, you must be born again. 'Verily, verily' — truly, truly." — And whenever He uses that formula He is always saying something of unusual seriousness and of deep import. He says, "Verily, verily, I say unto thee, Except [unless] a man be born again, he cannot see the kingdom of God."

This is the crucial phrase, the key phrase of Christianity: "Born again"! Some people say it should be translated "born from above". Others say it should be translated "born anew". I think that they are probably nearest to the truth who say that undoubtedly our Lord was speaking to Nicodemus in Aramaic, that the Greek is a translation from the Aramaic, and that then our English is a translation from the Greek. But the original was probably Aramaic, and there it means "except a man has another birth, he will never see the kingdom of God." It is the same thing. "Born again", "another birth", "born from above", "born of the Spirit" — take any of the terms you like.

This is the great New Testament doctrine and what it means, negatively, is that Christianity is not just an addition to something you have already got. It means that when people become Christians, it is not a little bit of improvement on what they were before; that what men and women need is not some new ideas to supplement the ideas that they already hold; they do not need a little extra added on to their thinking. Christianity, in other words, is not something that you and I, as we are, can take up; all that is contradicted here.

That is why our Lord interrupts Nicodemus. He is in that position; he says, "Look here, I am a ruler of the Jews, a master of Israel, I want this extra; I want everything I can get. I am a student and I am a teacher and thus everything new I see I want..." "Silence!" says our Lord. "You cannot add anything; you must be 'born again', you have nothing at all; you need a new foundation; you are not living, you are dead, you need to be born." That is His teaching negatively and it is all implicit here.

Then, here it is positively. Before we can become Christians we need an entirely new start. We do not start from where we are, we have to go down first. We can illustrate this from our modern cities. We see these new buildings going up; yes but before these went up, something else was pulled down. Demolition! Erection! And what is emphasised here is demolition. All we have is no good, it has got to be done away with, and pulled down, and then you begin to build. It is a new building. What we need is not a new coat of paint and a few window panes, and a new roof here and there. No, start afresh! "You have nothing to build on," says our Lord; "you have nothing to add to; what you need is comparable rather to being born again, a starting absolutely *de novo*, as if there had never been anything there before. It is like a birth."

And this is the New Testament teaching; sometimes it is called "a new creation", "regeneration"—you are generated anew and afresh. And, of course, by that He means that what you are by nature is useless and hopeless, that you need to be "a new man". So you need life, a new nature. God does not renovate us; He does not improve us or make us a little bit better. No, He puts new life into us. He works an operation on the soul and He infuses a principle of life, a new disposition— we are made "partakers of the divine nature."

"If any man be in Christ," says the Apostle Paul to the Corinthians, "he is a new creature [a new creation]; old things are passed away; behold, all things are become new" (2 Cor

5:17). He has a new outlook and understanding; new desires lie within him; he does not know himself. He is a new creation. He is like a man who is suddenly born and who says, "I was not there before, what has happened?"

But, secondly, our Lord says that this must happen to "all" men. This is most important. Remember, He is speaking to Nicodemus. John is careful to give us an introduction: "There was a man of the Pharisees named Nicodemus, a ruler of the Jews." Now that tells us a great deal about him; that it is to this man of all men that our Lord says, "You must be born again." We would not be surprised if He had said that to the Publicans, would we? They were the refuse of society. We would not have been surprised if He had said that to that poor prostitute who came and washed His feet with her tears, and wiped them with the hair of her head. We would understand it if He had said to her, "Woman, you need a new nature, you need a new start, a new life." But He said it to Nicodemus!

And there is only one thing to deduce from that. No one can enter the kingdom of God as they are; everybody must be "born again"—even a Nicodemus! There he is, a Pharisee, a teacher, a highly religious man, an instructor in the way of righteousness. Not only that, the Pharisees believed in these things. They believed in the divine decrees of God, in man's moral accountability and immortality; they believed in the resurrection of the body, in the existence of spirits, and in rewards and punishments in the future life. They believed all that. They were highly religious, and they were orthodox on all those matters.

Not only that, I can tell you more about this man Nicodemus. He came to Jesus by night; and that is a very good point about him. If people want to come to Christ, then there is something good about them. Nicodemus was in the crowd in Jerusalem and he had been listening. His opening words show that. He says, in effect, "You know I have watched you, I have never seen or heard anything like it..." All this is greatly in his favour. He is attracted by Christ, he admires Him; he recognises the excellency of His teaching and that He is working miracles. And they are such remarkable miracles that it is clearly the finger of God! He says, "This is not a man, this man is a special instrument of God!" He has all that insight.

Now there were fools who looked at Christ and spat in His face, as there are people today who only use His name as an oath or a curse. There are people who know nothing about Him. But here is a man who is drawn to Him, and who even humbles himself to come to seek some help from Him. All this is in his favour, as well as that which is already true of him as a Pharisee, a ruler of the Jews and an instructor of the people.

But—and this is the point—even he must be born again; even he must go back and become a little child and start afresh; even he cannot see the kingdom of God, leave alone enter it. This is why our Lord interrupts Nicodemus; it is because he is so good and so excellent; it is because he is so self-confident in his powers and in what he can do. He comes, not exactly as an equal, but as a man who only just needs a little extra, he is not much below; and Christ has to demolish him, He has to put him on his back as it were, and convince him that he is nothing and nobody. So He does it in this dramatic manner.

There, then, is the first great fundamental principle—we must be born again. But let me come to the second. "Verily, verily, I say unto thee, Except a man be born again he cannot see the kingdom of God." Why? Why must we be born again? Well it is all put before us here with very great clarity. The first answer is, because we are what we are by nature. It is obvious, is it not? If I need a new life it is because there is something wrong with the one I have got.

Look at this as it is portrayed in Nicodemus. You see, we show what we are by the fact that all our ideas and all our thinking about these things are wrong. That was the essential trouble with Nicodemus. Look at his thought, look at his statement. His whole approach to the kingdom of God is entirely wrong. He comes with his presuppositions and he says, "I am glad to have heard you, I am glad to have seen those miracles. You know, this is the help I wanted, I think now I am going to get it from you." "Wrong!" says our Lord. "Stop! Keep silent! Listen, you have got nothing."

And we, too, have a curious notion that to be a Christian, is just to be a little bit better than we are now. We think that if we stop doing one or two things, and take up two or three others, then we are Christians. Is not that it? Knock off one bit, add on another! Put on a new suit, brighten up a bit, clean yourself a little bit...ah, and then you are all right. But that is not Christianity; that is morality if you like; ethical behaviour or philosophy. It is all right but it is not Christianity. It is as far removed from it as it can possibly be. No, all our thinking about this is wrong!

And we have seen that. That is why we often see so many monstrous statements in the Press and in other places, telling us that the people who are really practising the Christian life and advocating its cause today are some of the well-known infidels. That is simply because they object to atomic bombs perhaps, and that, people say, makes a man a Christian. How can we be further away in our thinking about the kingdom of God than that!

But let me show you something else. We need to be born again, because, as we are, we are quite incapable of spiritual thinking. That is always to me the striking thing in this particular incident. Nicodemus proves that to the very hilt. Do not forget, here is a Pharisee, a very great man, and an able one; obviously well taught and well instructed and an expert on the Jewish religion. And yet—let me put it quite simply—what an utter fool he makes of himself! How dull and stupid he is! What ridiculous things he says to our Lord! He is incapable of spiritual thinking.

Our Lord, interrupting him, says to him, "Verily, verily, I say unto thee, Except a man be born again, he cannot see the kingdom of God." This is one of the greatest spiritual announcements ever made, if not the greatest. Then, notice the response: "Nicodemus saith unto him, How can a man be born when he is old? can he enter the second time into his mother's womb, and be born?" Oh, he would even be a disgrace at

Speakers' Corner in Hyde Park, it is so monstrously ridiculous. What a foolish interruption! Our Lord makes this great spiritual pronouncement—and Nicodemus does not understand.

And then look at him as he goes on. "Jesus answered, Verily, verily, I say unto thee, Except a man be born of water and of the Spirit, he cannot enter into the kingdom of God." Then: "The wind bloweth where it listeth, thou hearest the sound thereof, but canst tell whence it cometh, nor whither it goeth: so is every one that is born of the Spirit. Nicodemus answered and said unto him, How can these things be?"—he is completely at sea, he still does not understand.

And yet he is but a typical man in all that. The Apostle Paul puts it in a very pregnant phrase. He says, "The natural man receiveth not the things of the Spirit of God; for they are foolishness unto him; neither can he know them, because they are spiritually discerned" (1 Cor 2:14). And modern men and women when they are confronted by this spiritual truth in the New Testament, say, "What on earth is all that about?" They do not understand it, they cannot follow it. They are utterly ignorant. It does not matter how clever they are. I do not care if they are the greatest philosophers in the land; if you put these two things before them, they fumble as obviously as Nicodemus did.

Why is this? The full explanation is given here. "Nicodemus," says our Lord, "you cannot follow me. You think I am talking about a man being born physically the second time. But I am not talking about physical things but about spiritual things: 'That which is born of the Spirit is spirit.' That is what I am talking about. 'Marvel not that I said unto thee, Ye must be born again.' "

"But," our Lord continues, "you know why you cannot follow? It is because you are in the flesh, and 'that which is born of the flesh is flesh', it cannot rise above itself, it cannot do anything but reproduce its own nature; that is why I say that you must be born again. You see, Nicodemus, you cannot even think in my categories; you are living in a different realm altogether. You are like a man who is born deaf trying to understand music, or like a blind man trying to be a critic of art. You are incapable, because your nature is wrong."

The Apostle Paul, having learned, of course, from the Master, puts it like this: "The carnal mind is enmity against God; for it is not subject to the law of God, neither indeed can be" (Rom 8:7). This is why people are not Christian. Poor blind people, they cannot help it; they have a carnal fleshly nature, and it is something that is against God. The carnal mind is not only dull and blind and stupid, it is "enmity against God". It hates God, it reviles Him. The Apostle says in another place, "In me, (that is in my flesh,) dwelleth no good thing" (Rom 7:18). Or indeed our Lord puts it still more plainly in verse 19 of this chapter, "This is the condemnation, that light is come [or has come] into the world, and men loved darkness rather than light, because their deeds were evil."

And that is where these modern teachers go so wrong, with all their ideas and statements as to how present day men and women should be approached with the Gospel. As we have seen, they speak as if the problem were an intellectual one. But it is not. "This is the condemnation, that light has come into the world..." Why do people not turn to it? Why do they not believe it and accept it? Oh, our Lord says, "men loved darkness rather than light because their deeds were evil." I will tell you why they do not believe in Christ: it is because they love fornication and adultery; because they love evil; their hearts are rotten, they are haters of God. "That which is born of the flesh is flesh"—and it will never rise above its own level and its own nature. That is why we need to be born again; our natures are opposed to the truth of God, and therefore we need new ones.

But let me give you a second reason, which is much more important. We need to be born again not only because we are what we are, but also because the kingdom of God is what it is. It is "the kingdom *of God*"! Not the kingdom of Socrates, or Plato or Aristotle. Not the kingdom of music, of Mozart, or of Beethoven...No, it is the kingdom of God! It is not something external, it is something spiritual. "The kingdom of God is within you" (Lk 17:21). It is not a morality or a correct code of behaviour. No, it is entering into the spiritual realm, into fellowship with the almighty and the everlasting God. It means being a citizen of God's kingdom, it means walking with Him.

And, remember, "God is light, and in him is no darkness at all" (1 Jn 1:5). The Psalmist understood this: "Who shall ascend into the hill of the Lord?" he says, "or who shall stand in his holy place? He that hath clean hands, and a pure heart; who hath not lifted up his soul unto vanity, nor sworn deceitfully" (Ps 24:3–4). This is a realm of personal relationship, not one of views and of ideas, and of opposition. No, it means that you enjoy spiritual communion with God; you speak to Him and He speaks to you. The old relationship that obtained between God and Adam and Eve is restored and you become a companion of God; you are an heir of God, and you live in the realm of the spiritual.

But this is the problem. How can one dwell with such a God and have communion with Him? The Apostle says to the Corinthians, "Be ye not unequally yoked together with unbelievers"—Why? For this reason: "What fellowship hath righteousness with unrighteousness? and what communion hath light with darkness? And what concord hath Christ with Belial? or what part hath he that believeth with an infidel? And what agreement hath the temple of God with idols? for ye are the temple of the living God; as God hath said, I will dwell in them, and walk in them; and I will be their God, and they shall be my people" (2 Cor 6:14–16). That is what it means to be in the kingdom of God!

> There is a city bright;
> Closed are its gates to sin;
>   Nought that defileth,
>   Nought that defileth
> Can ever enter in.
>
> Mary Ann Sanderson Deck

It is the realm of light and of glory; and before I can enter it I must have something in me that corresponds to that.

But it is not only the nature of the kingdom, it is the whole question of God's purpose and God's thought and plan. This is why we need to be born again. God has put this very plainly through the mouth of the prophet Isaiah in chapter 55. He says, "My thought are not your thoughts, neither are your ways my ways, saith the Lord. For as the heavens are higher than the earth, so are my ways higher than your ways, and my thoughts than your thoughts" (Is 55:8–9). Look at this fool, Nicodemus—what else can I call him—pitting his little puny, physical, carnal mind, his mind of flesh, against such a truth, the mind of God and the purpose of God.

It is all put before us here so plainly. "Nicodemus answered and said unto him, How can these things be? Jesus answered and said unto him, Art thou a master of Israel, and knowest not these things? Verily, verily, I say unto thee, We speak that we do know, and testify that we have seen; and ye receive not our witness. If I have told you earthly things, and ye believe not, how shall ye believe, if I tell you of heavenly things?" (vv 9–12). "Man," He says in effect, "listen; you must be born again, because I am talking about heavenly things. I am not talking about the stuff you can read in the newspapers, nor about mathematics that you can study and master with your mind. I am not even giving you poetry—man at the highest flight of his imagination. No, I am giving you heavenly things! The things of God! You cannot rise to them. Do not try to; you must be born again."

And what are these heavenly things, these thoughts of God? "No man hath ascended up to heaven, but he that came down from heaven, even the Son of man which is in heaven" (v 13). Do you know what that means? Nicodemus does not—and there he is trying to understand. He thinks that he does understand this man of whom he is seeking an interview; a wonderful teacher, he says the greatest of us all!

Yes but he thinks He is only a man, and our Lord points out to him here that He is not. He says, "Nicodemus, I am talking to you on earth but I am still in heaven! I am the Son of Man! Can you follow that sort of thing? Is your mind adequate? Of course it is not, that is why you need to be born again." This is the word being made flesh! This is the miracle of God becoming man! This is the Virgin Birth! This is all the glory of the incarnation! Where is the mind that can understand it?

But our Lord goes on: "And as Moses lifted up the serpent in the wilderness, even so must the Son of man be lifted up: That whosoever believeth in Him should not perish, but have eternal life. For God so loved the world, that he gave his only begotten Son, that whosoever believeth in him should not perish, but have everlasting life" (vv 14–16). "Now then," says our Lord, "Do you understand it?" How do men and women become Christians? How are they saved? How do they enter into the kingdom of God? They put in an effort, they live a better life, they attend a place of worship? No! There is only one way. The Son of Man must come down and must be lifted up as the serpent was lifted up in the wilderness.

And this is the thing that the natural man, the man who is in the flesh, can never accept and never understand. "There is only one way whereby anybody can be saved," says Christ, "and that is that I die for him. As that brazen serpent was lifted up of old in the wilderness, and everybody who had been bitten by a snake had but to look at him and he was healed, so I have got to be lifted up. I have got to bear the punishment of sin, and anybody who looks to me and believes in me is saved." That is the message! But "the preaching of the cross is to them that perish foolishness," says Paul (1 Cor 1:18). It still is, it always has been. "The Jews require a sign, and the Greeks seek after wisdom; but we preach Christ crucified, unto the Jews a stumblingblock and unto the Greeks foolishness" (1 Cor 1:22– 23). And it still is! Man cannot understand it; he says, "It is immoral that one should die for all. It is impossible! I cannot get it. I must save myself." But no, this is the way and the natural man hates it and rejects it.

Then add to that this whole matter of regeneration—men and women being born again, having a new nature, though they may be old, perhaps tottering at the side of the grave; they can start anew, and receive a new life. That is the nature of the kingdom and its teaching, and the natural man cannot receive it; he needs, therefore, to be born again.

And that brings me to my last principle which is this: how can a man be born again? How does it ever become possible? And that, too, is all here. It is obviously, patently, nothing that you and I can do. You cannot give birth to yourself; you cannot change your nature. You cannot become as a little child, you cannot start anew, you would if you could; but you cannot. It is impossible. No, we must be born again; we must be born from above, we must be born of the Spirit.

It is the great act of God. "The wind bloweth where it listeth, and thou hearest the sound thereof, but canst not tell whence it cometh, and whither it goeth: so is every one that is born of the Spirit" (Jn 3:8). It is a great mystery because it is a miracle. Indeed it has all been stated already at the beginning of John's Gospel: "But as many as received him, to them gave he power to become the sons of God, even to them that believe on his name: Which were born, not of blood, nor of the will of the flesh, nor of the will of man, but of God" (Jn 1:12–13). The new nature can only be made by God. It is His gift. It is the God who made us making us again.

Oh, I do not understand it; it is like the wind! You see the effects, you hear it when it strikes you, but you do not understand, there is a mystery. It is there, it comes, it goes, it does things, but you cannot fathom it—"So is every one that is born of the Spirit." A man finds himself a new man. People say, "Something has happened to me, I see things I never saw; I feel, I know: What is this?" They do not know, but they know it has happened. It is the recreating act of God. They have been smashed, they have been restored, they have been re-made. They know they are new men and women in Christ Jesus.

"Can we do nothing?" you say. Well, you can. I will tell you what you can do. You can recognise your need of it. "Except a man be born of water and of the Spirit, he cannot enter the kingdom of God" (v 5). "Born of water" is baptism, if you like, repentance. It is a man or woman saying, "I see now that I am blind; I am vile and foul; I need to be cleansed, I cannot stand before God, I need to be washed, I need to be renewed." That is repentance!

You must further acknowledge that you can do nothing about it. You must cast yourself upon the mercy of God as a suppliant, as a helpless, hopeless pauper. You must cast yourself upon His mercy and ask Him to have forgiveness upon you and to receive you and to give you life anew. You must cease to try to understand. "Marvel not that I said unto thee, Ye must be born again." Recognise that it is the heavenly truth and the heavenly things of God. Recognise your smallness, your finite capacity, your ignorance. Give up, give in. Confess it, though you are a great man in Israel. Repent, believe, and leave yourselves in the Almighty and loving hands of God.

Believe on the name of the Son of God; believe this one who confronted Nicodemus and who interrupted him and said, "Stop! You have nothing and I have got everything to give you. 'For God so loved the world that he gave his only begotten Son that whosoever believeth in him should not perish, but have everlasting life.' "

12 A KINGDOM WHICH CANNOT BE MOVED

See that ye refuse not him that speaketh. For if they escaped not who refused him that spake on earth, much more shall not we escape, if we turn away from him that speaketh from heaven: Whose voice then shook the earth: but now he hath promised, saying, Yet once more I shake not the earth only, but also heaven. And this word, Yet once more, signifieth the removing of those things that are shaken, as of things that are made, that those things which cannot be shaken may remain. Wherefore we receiving a kingdom which cannot be moved, let us have grace, whereby we may serve God acceptably with reverence and godly fear: For our God is a consuming fire (Heb 12:25–29).

WE NOW COME TO OUR FINAL WORD in this series on the kingdom of God; only one thing remains to be said, and that is: "See that ye refuse not him that speaketh." Or to put it in the form of a question, Have we heard what the Lord Jesus Christ has got to say? Have we heard His teaching about the kingdom of God and the only way whereby it can be entered? The word has come to us, it is the word of the New Testament, and the question is—what have we done about it? It calls for a response and an acceptance, so have we received it? Have we laid hold upon it and acted upon it? Have we made certain that we have sought and found the kingdom, and have entered into it?

Now this, according to the whole of the teaching of the New Testament, is a most vital, urgent matter; it comes out here in this man's word, "See that ye refuse not him that speaketh. For if they escaped not who refused him that spake on earth, much more shall not we escape, if we turn away from him that speaketh from heaven."

So have we realised the urgency of entering the kingdom of God? Have we realised that this is the most vital question for every one of us? You remember the words of our Lord? "Seek ye first the kingdom of God and his righteousness." Have we done so? It has been opened out before us, the truth about the kingdom and the way of entry into it and we cannot hear this message and ever be the same again. Every one of us who has ever heard it has either accepted it or else refused it because there are no other positions. We cannot be neutral about this matter. To receive it means that we enter into the kingdom, and we know that we have done so. It is something of which people are conscious, something in which they rejoice.

In these verses, then, the writer to the Hebrews having, in his way, given his teaching concerning the kingdom of God, now comes to the end of his letter. He has a few practical things to say in the thirteenth chapter but this is really the end of the epistle. So having displayed the great doctrine, he says, "Now then, see that ye refuse not him that speaketh." And I, too, would say the same thing.

But why should we all pay "the most earnest heed" to this; why should we give it the greatest attention possible and really do something about it? Well, the writer gives us the answers, and the first is that we should listen to this New Testament message, this preaching of the Christian Gospel and its content, because of the one who is speaking it, because of the one who has given it to us—"See that ye refuse not *him that speaketh*." Now here is a point which we must never lose sight of. This is what makes the preaching of the Gospel so utterly unique and entirely different from everything else that is ever happening in the world.

The world as it is today is confronted by large numbers of people who claim that they can answer the questions and that they have the solution to our problems. I am not here to criticise such people, but what I would say about them all is that they are only men. They are all the ideas and the theories of men. The thing that puts this message in a category entirely on its own is "Him that speaketh". This is the Word of God! It is not a human idea, not a human proposal, not man trying to solve the problem. This writer constantly says that: "God," he says at the very beginning of his letter, "who at sundry times and in divers manners spake in times past unto the fathers by the prophets, Hath in these last days spoken unto us by his Son..." (Heb 1:1-2). There it is. It is God speaking!

Does not this at once make this matter very urgent? We are no longer looking at the nostrums of men, or at their various ideas; here is something that claims that it is a word from God Himself. God spoke to the fathers through the prophets; the Old Testament is the word of God. You cannot explain the story of the Children of Israel in any other terms, but that God was speaking to them and giving them a message and showing them His way. And they realised that and that is why they were the people that they were.

But if that is true of the Old Testament, how much more is it true of the New? The whole of Christianity depends on the fact that something has happened in history. This is what makes this Gospel unique. Jesus of Nazareth is a historical figure. It is no longer a question of looking at a great number of teachers and evaluating which is the best and the greatest and the highest. No, here is one who claims that He is in a category entirely on His own. What differentiates Christianity from all the so-called great religions and all the philosophies of the world is simply this: that more important than the teaching is the Teacher.

Primarily, Christianity is not a view of life, it is an account of something that has been done. Christianity is a historical religion. It is not just a good idea as to how to live, nor a programme for living; it is more than that. It is an announcement and a proclamation of what God has *done*. It is God, the Bible says at the beginning, who "created the heaven and the earth", and the sea, and all that is in them. It is God who has constantly been visiting His people. And the essence of the Gospel, as we have seen, is this: "When the fulness of the time was come, God sent forth his Son, made of a woman, made under the law, to redeem them that were under the law" (Gal 4:4–5). God "hath visited and redeemed his people" (Lk 1:68).

In other words, we can put it like this: the uniqueness of this message lies in the fact that there has been one in this world who really did not belong to it. The world has thrown up its great men, its great philosophers, its great scientists, its great statesmen and great musicians and many other great men, but Jesus of Nazareth was not a great man, He was God-Man!

This is the appalling thing, is it not, that two thousand years later, He is still being ignored. The world has always been a place of trouble and of pain, and the whole story of civilization is that of the human race trying to solve its own problems. Read the history of Greece, and the works of its great philosophers. Read the history of Rome and the great Roman lawgivers— those marvellous men who were experts in imperial and local government—what where they doing?

Well, they were all trying to solve the problem of the human race, trying to put an end to war, trying to make people live amicably together, trying to order life so that men and women might live it as it should be lived and that they might enjoy it. But they all failed yet the world is still trying, still turning to the same kind of idea, still looking back to Greek philosophy and so on. And mankind today is doing everything except listening to this one thing.

That is why this writer puts it like this: "See that ye refuse not him that speaketh." God has spoken to us in His Son at that crucial turning-point of history. God the eternal Son left the courts of Heaven and He entered into this world! Have you come face to face with this fact? Have you faced the phenomenon of Jesus of Nazareth? Have you looked at Him, have you listened to Him? Who is He? Is He just a man to you? Is He just one of the great teachers or do you recognise that here "the Word was made flesh and dwelt amongst us" (Jn 1:14). Do you recognise that God has come out of Heaven into time, into this world, in order to solve the problem of the world?

I am not here representing a human teaching. Here is my basis, that verse that we were looking at in the last study: "God so loved the world, that he gave his only begotten Son, that whosoever believeth in him should not perish but have everlasting life." I preach this gospel for this one reason only, that it is God's own way of salvation, and if we had no other reason than that for considering it, that is enough in and of itself.

Now if you have not accepted that, you are refusing it. Is your whole life based upon what God has spoken in His Son? Do you realise that God has spoken to you about yourself and your problems, and about your need and the way to solve it? that God has spoken to you about the whole world, about life, death and eternity: "Him that speaketh"! We are listening to the word of the living God!

But the writer has a second reason for pressing it upon us: "Whose voice then shook the earth, but now he hath promised, saying, Yet once more I shake not the earth only but also heaven. And this word, Yet once more, signifieth the removing of those things that are shaken, as of things that are made, that those things which cannot be shaken may remain."

What does this mean? Well, he is here contrasting the old dispensation with the new. He is writing to Hebrew Christians and he is reminding them how the law was given to them by God through Moses on that great and famous occasion on Mount Sinai. He says, "Look back at that, consider that," and he gives them this tremendous description of it. He says, "For ye are not come unto the mount that might be touched, and that burned with fire, nor unto blackness, and darkness, and tempest, And the sound of a trumpet, and the voice of words; which voice they that heard intreated that the word should not be spoken to them any more: (For they could not endure that which was commanded,—the command was that—if so much as a beast touched the mountain, it shall be stoned, or thrust through with a dart: And so terrible was the sight that Moses said, I exceedingly fear and quake:)." But you have not come to that, he says, "Ye are come unto mount Sion, and unto the city of the living God, the heavenly Jerusalem, and to an innumerable company of angels, To the general assembly and church of the firstborn, which are written in heaven"—and notice!—"and to God the Judge of all" (Heb 12:18–23).

Here again is the great basic theme of the whole of the Bible. Why should I listen to this New Testament message? I must listen to it because I am moving every day I live nearer and nearer to a final judgment. "God, the Judge of all!" It is here from the beginning of the Bible to the very end. The writer sums it up at the end of the ninth chapter when he puts it like this: "As it is appointed unto men once to die, but after this the judgment: So Christ was once offered to bear the sins of many; and unto them that look for him shall he appear the second time without sin unto salvation" (vv 27–28).

So the second reason for listening to the Gospel is simply that I am reminded by this message everywhere that my life in this world is nothing but a pilgrimage, nothing but a journey. How difficult it is to realise that! We are so accustomed to trying to settle down in life, and everything seems to go on in the same way, year after year, and though the years pass so rapidly, we do not realise the meaning and the significance of it all. But we are nothing but journeymen, "strangers and pilgrims"; we are all travellers and sojourners. It is true of all of us that we are "here today and gone tomorrow."

But over and above that is the fact that, according to the Bible, men and women are responsible beings; they have been made in the image of God; they have been made like God, and God has endowed them with these great faculties in order that they might live in this world to His glory. And everyone of us is going to be held responsible for that. Judgment is the great note of the Bible. All along we are asked to consider that fact, that we will have to stand before God and give an account of the deeds done in the body, whether they are good or bad. Everybody has got to stand before God who is "the Judge of all".

Now when God made man at the beginning He made it quite clear to him that He was putting him on probation; He told him what to do and what not to do, and He told him the consequences of disobeying His own holy law. The whole of man's life in this world has been lived in terms of his relationship to God, and this tremendous fact of the Judgment.

But this is the thing that the modern world, of course, never stops to think about at all. We have got hold of this theory of evolution—which is nothing but a theory—that man has evolved out of the animal and that he lives and dies and there is the end of him. But according to the Bible that is the lie of the devil, and that is what makes the listening to this Gospel such an urgent matter. Of course, if man when he dies, finishes, if that is the end of all, and if, when men die, they just disappear, like a flower dying or an animal, then, of course, there is no need to preach the Gospel. The Gospel is not primarily meant to do things for us in this world. It does do things for us here, as we shall see, but that is not the primary reason for the Gospel.

The first reason for the Gospel is this fact that every one of us will stand before God in the Judgment. God is the Judge of all! And here, in these verses, we are told something about the character of God. Notice the end of this statement, "Our God is a consuming fire." By this he means that God is holy; that God is righteous, and pure, and just. He constantly says this; he does so in chapter 10 verse 31: "It is a fearful thing to fall into the hands of the living God."

The trouble with the world today is not that people do not believe in the Lord Jesus Christ; it is that they do not believe in God. And they do not believe in Christ, because they do not believe in God. It is no use saying to people, "Come to Jesus." They say, "Why should I come to Jesus? I do not need your Jesus, everything is all right with me, I am having a very good time, I have never been happier." And they do not come! You can appeal to them but they do not pay the slightest attention, and this is because they do not believe in God, they do not believe in the judgment and they do not believe in a future life. They cannot prove it, they just say it. They are fools enough to risk all upon their own ignorance and their own theories. But the Bible says, "See that ye refuse not him that speaketh." Why? Because He is the very one who is going to judge you.

Now this man gives us some conception of that. When God gave the law to the Children of Israel through Moses, He gave it on the top of Mount Sinai, and here is the description of that. The people were terrified. They were not allowed to go up on to the mount, they were at its foot. They were not even allowed to touch it; anybody who touched it was put to death and any animal that touched it was stoned. And suddenly there was a tremendous manifestation from Heaven, there was fire and thunder and an earthquake, and the sounding of a trumpet.

It is all described in most graphic terms in Exodus 19. "And when the voice of the trumpet sounded long, and waxed louder and louder, Moses spake, and God answered him by a voice..." (v 19). "And mount Sinai was altogether on a smoke, because the Lord descended upon it in fire: and the smoke thereof ascended as the smoke of a furnace, and the whole mount quaked greatly" (v 18). The mountain was literally trembling because God had come down upon it.

This is a figure, an emblem; it is a manifestation of the power of God, and the glory of God, and His holiness. He is a "consuming fire"! "God is light, and him is no darkness at all" (1 Jn 1:5). Have you ever visualised yourself standing before Him? That is what you will have to do.

Then there is another similar statement in the account of the last judgment in Matthew 24:29: "Immediately after the tribulation of those days shall the sun be darkened, and the moon shall not give her light, and the stars shall fall from heaven, and the powers of the heavens shall be shaken." It is the same as the verse in our passage: "Yet once more I shake not the earth only, but also heaven." Oh, how difficult it is for us to realise these things; but as certainly as we are men and women, alive today, we have got to face God in the Judgment—every one of us.

The whole Bible is concerned about this. This is why Christ

came into the world; not merely to make us feel happy, not merely to heal our bodies and to give us a good time here. No, it is to put us right with God, because He is our Judge and He is a holy Judge. He is one who "shakes". He shakes men, He shakes the universe, He will shake the very heavens. "Whose voice," he says, "then shook the earth: For if they escaped not who refused him that spake on earth, much more shall not we escape, if we turn away from him that speaketh from heaven."

Which being interpreted means this. God gave His law to Moses, and through Moses to the Children of Israel. He said, "I am a holy God, a jealous God, and the important thing in life for you is to please me. If you do, I will bless you, but if you do not I will punish you"—". . . visiting the iniquity of the fathers upon the children unto the third and fourth generation of them that hate me" (Ex 20:5).

God said that, and He did it. He gave that law to His own people, whom He had brought out of the captivity of Egypt and to whom He had promised the land of Canaan. But did you know that all the adults, every one of them except two, died in the wilderness and never got to Canaan at all? Why not? Because they sinned, because they rebelled, because they did not receive the word of God. They were His own people, His own chosen people, they were the people to whom He had given these great promises and whom He had blessed in such a signal manner; but even they, because they disobeyed, died in the wilderness, all except Caleb and Joshua. God carries out what He says he will do.

I will tell you more. Look at Moses; look at this great man of God, this man whom God spoke to "face to face", this man who was the appointed leader, and who was blessed in such an extraordinary manner. Do you remember this about the story of Moses—he was not allowed to enter into the land of Canaan, the promised land, himself. He was the man to whom the honour was given of leading the people out of Egypt, across the Red Sea and through the wilderness, right up to the verge of Jordan—and then he was taken! It was because he had disobeyed God. God told him to "speak to the rock" but instead of that he struck it. And because of that he was not allowed the great and the high privilege of leading the people across Jordan into the promised land.

Read the Old Testament history. God said, "This is my law, I am carrying it out." And He did carry it out. He never failed. The Law was never allowed to fail. "So, listen," says this writer; "if that was true then, how much more is it true now." Here then is our second great reason for listening to this Gospel; that we are all moving in the direction of this final judgment. There is a day coming, when this whole universe will be "shaken". It is not as difficult to believe that now, as it used to be, is it? People used to laugh at the idea that the heavens and the earth would pass away, and that "the elements" would "melt with fervent heat" (2 Pet 3:10). "Ah," they said, "that is the nonsense of the Scripture; you people believe in a flood, and you believe that the world will be burnt up at the end. You are children," they said, "when will you grow up and have some sense; when will you be scientific?"

Well, if you are scientific today you do not have much difficulty in believing that the elements shall melt with a fervent heat! Atomic physics has taught us to believe that the world can be shaken. Even when they let off these experimental bombs, instruments which detect these things show us that there is a tremor through the whole world. And what we are told here is that God will shake the whole universe. Everything that man glories in and takes pride in will be shaken to the dust.

> "And, like the baseless fabric of this vision,
> The cloud-capp'd towers, the gorgeous palaces,
> The solemn temples, the great globe itself,
> Yes, all which it inherit, shall dissolve..."

it will all disintegrate and disappear.

Our Lord once said to the people, "I am not going to judge you," "I came not to judge the world" (Jn 12:47). "But," He said, "there is one that judgeth you." What is that? "The word that I have spoken, the same shall judge him in the last day" (Jn

12:48). In other words it comes to this, that you have been told about the judgment and you have seen the terms of the judgment. It means standing before the God who made you, the God who has told you how to live, the God who has told you to live to His glory and who wants you to love Him with all your heart and mind and soul and strength, and your neighbour as yourself. And the one question He will ask you is this: Did you do so? Did you live to me and to my glory? Or did you live to the pride of life of the world and to its drink and its gambling and its sex and its enjoyment—what did you live for? Those are the terms in which we shall be judged.

Then, the writer gives a third reason for listening to this Gospel, which is that this is the only way whereby we shall be able to stand in that judgment. There is only one way to be right with God and ready for that judgment, it is this: it is not to refuse Him that speaketh but to listen to Him and to believe Him and to act upon what He says, and to enter into the kingdom of God. It is the only way. Now that is put here like this: "Yet once more I shake not the earth only, but also heaven. And this word, Yet once more, signifieth the removing of those things that are shaken, as of things that are made, that those things which cannot be shaken may remain."

He is, as we have seen, talking about the law that was given through Moses. "You have not come back again to that," he says in effect. "Do you know that even the law of Moses has been put on one side; it has been removed, and superseded." The law of Moses was only a temporary measure and all the ecclesiastical arrangements of the ancient Israelites, were but a temporary expedient, "things that are made".

This is a tremendous thing. All that has been shaken, it has gone. The Temple has gone, the burnt offerings and sacrifices, the priests and the high priest—they have all gone, temporary measures. There is only one thing left and that is the Gospel of the Lord Jesus Christ.

The New English Bible has got a good translation here; it translates it like this: "The words once again—and only once." God through the prophet Haggai said, "I am going to speak again, I am going to shake 'once more', and only once, never another one. I will do away with the law, and the Temple; I will do away with the burnt offerings and sacrifices. All that is going, I am going to put in something else and that is the last; there will be nothing after that" (Hag 2). "Once again, and only once" because it is once and for ever.

Here is the great reason for believing the Gospel—that it is the only way whereby we can be prepared for the judgment of God and made safe. This is God's last word, God's final provision—"Once"! Never again! Nothing will supersede this Gospel. It is God's last word to the human race. And this is the argument, that if God has put on one side even His own Law and removed it, how much more will the theories and the thinking and the philosophies of men be put on one side! If His own Law has been shaken away, everything else will be shaken away, there is nothing left but this.

This is the blessed news of the Gospel. "You have not come to the mount that might be touched, and that burned"—what have you come to then?—"But you are come unto Mount Sion, and to the city of the living God, to the heavenly Jerusalem, and to an innumerable company of angels, To the general assembly and church of the firstborn...And to *Jesus the mediator of the new covenant*." And, he goes on to say, "to the blood of sprinkling, that speaketh better things than that of Abel."

Let me explain. There is a new covenant, which has come in Jesus; He is "the mediator of a new covenant." God is holding out an offer to the human race! This Almighty God who is going to judge us all and who is over all, He is extending a new opportunity, a new covenant, the last covenant, the last offer; and He has sent it in His Son. Not in a servant, not in a prophet, not in a priest. No, His own Son came out of heaven into this world, "Jesus, the Son of God"!

The old covenant said, "Do this, and you shall live." Do what? "Love the Lord your God with the whole of your being." "Do not commit adultery, do not kill, do not steal, do not bear false witness" and all the rest of it. "Which if a man do, he shall live in them" (Lev 18:5). And no one could do it—no one. But here is the Mediator of a new covenant. "Believe on the Lord Jesus Christ and thou shalt be saved." Why? Well because of "the blood of sprinkling"!

Here is the theme of eternity. We are all wretched, we are all foul. What if the world knew your imaginations and your thought; what if you neighbours knew the things that you fondle in your heart? We are all vile, lost sinners, but we have got to stand before a holy God who is a "consuming fire". How can we do it? What about the stains on your soul, what about the chastity and the purity you have lost, what about the foulness that has entered into you...What will you do about it? How will you remove it and erase it? And you cannot!

But here is a new covenant, mediated by the Son of God. He has shed His precious blood on the Cross on Calvary's hill,

> His blood can make the foulest clean,
> His blood availed for me.
> Charles Wesley

We see this in Hebrews 10:19–22: "Having therefore, brethren, boldness to enter into the holiest by the blood of Jesus, By a new and living way, which he hath consecrated for us, through the veil, that is to say, his flesh; And having an high priest over the house of God; Let us draw near with a true heart in full assurance of faith, having our hearts sprinkled"—*sprinkled*—"from an evil conscience..." How can I approach God in prayer, that holy God who is a "consuming fire", when I know that I am sinful and damned; how can I go with confidence? Here is the answer: Get the sprinkling of the blood of Christ upon your heart and your conscience.

It means, as we have seen, that you believe that your sins were laid upon Him, and that God sent Him into this world to bear your sins in His own body on the tree. This writer puts it like this: "We see Jesus, who was made a little lower than the angels for the suffering of death...that he by the grace of God should taste death for every man." Here is the new message about the new Mediator, that whatever your sins are, Christ died for your sins! Believe that and His blood will be sprinkled upon you. "Jesus, the mediator of the new covenant", will purge your conscience, He will cleanse your soul and you will have nothing to fear in the judgment.

But let me give you my last reason why we must not refuse Him that speaketh. It is because of the glories of the kingdom into which this Christ introduces us. "Wherefore we receiving a kingdom which cannot be moved..." Here it is, thank God for it. What a privilege to preach such a Gospel!

Look at it like this: What are the blessings of the kingdom?—I have already mentioned some of them. You get some of the blessings of this kingdom immediately in this world. Firstly, forgiveness! What a wonderful thing to know that all my sins are blotted out! I am no longer held responsible for the things I have done—Christ has borne them for me! I am forgiven! Oh, the wonder of such a knowledge! Have you got it? If you have not got it, it is because you "refuse him that speaketh". He is telling you about a "blood of sprinkling that speaketh better things than that of Abel." And what it speaks, as I have been showing you, is that the moment you believe in Him you are already forgiven, completely and absolutely!

Not only that; you are reconciled to God. You have access into His presence; "Having therefore, brethren, boldness to enter into the holiest..."—that is it!—able to speak to God and to have communion and fellowship with Him. More: you become a child of God. Did you notice this: "Ye are come unto mount Sion, unto the city of the living God, the heavenly Jerusalem, and to an innumerable company of angels, To the general assembly, and *church of the firstborn*."

That is the blessing! Every man or woman who is a true Christian and a true member of the Christian church is one of God's "firstborn". That means two things; it means that you are born again, you become a child of God—yes, but also everybody in the Christian Church is a firstborn child. This means that you are an heir. The first born is the heir and he has the peculiar privileges of that position. "Israel," says God in the Old Testament, "is my son, my firstborn." And everyone who is a Christian is a firstborn child of God. Here, we are all joint heirs with Christ, no one more than another, and we become heirs of all that God has got for us. And while we are left in this world of time we enjoy the special favour of our Father and receive His blessings day by day. That is in this world.

And what in the next world? Well it is glory! It is to be with Him, it is to be like Him, it is to reign with Christ as kings and as priests. "Know ye not," says Paul to the Corinthians, "that the saints shall judge the world...Know ye not that we shall judge angels?" (1 Cor 6:2–3). Christian people do you realise these things? Nobody else realises them. Men and women are in the world today because they know nothing about the glory that is coming. City life! "What a thrill I get out of it!" they say, "the kicks, the enjoyment!" But they will soon be lying on their deathbed and they will not be able to enjoy it; they will be leaving it, and they will have nothing, it will all be shaken, and they will be shaken. And here is the glory that they have refused. That is why men and women are not Christians; they know nothing about this glory; being with God and being with Christ and reigning with Him, and triumphing with Him and enjoying Him to all eternity. The blessings of the kingdom!

And then, there is the safety and the security of the kingdom: "We receiving a kingdom which cannot be moved." Everything else can be removed; there is nothing stable in this world. People used to think the British Empire was stable— how much of it is left? Those everlasting mountains—stable? Of course they are not. They are moving the whole time and an earthquake can wreck them, a bomb can smash them. Nothing is stable. The whole world will be convulsed in a final cataclysm, nothing will remain. But here is a kingdom which cannot be moved.

Is this true? Well, history proves it. Christ said, "The gates of hell shall not prevail against it" (Mt 16:18), and they have not. People have been dying ever since He founded the Church, but the Church goes on. All the enemies have risen throughout the centuries; Herod tried to end it, so did the Roman Empire, and others have tried to do the same. The Christian Church has always been under the heel of tyranny and oppression but she goes on. Why? Well because she cannot be shaken, she cannot be moved.

That is the story of the past and it is true today. I am not afraid of Communism or of any other 'ism. All the modern theories will be forgotten; nobody will know about them; they will vanish into thin air and the Church will go on and the Gospel will yet be proclaimed, and this will be true always. "No weapon that is formed against thee shall prosper" (Is 54:17). This is a kingdom that "cannot be moved". Daniel the Prophet saw it. He saw great kingdoms arising; they were great, they were made of gold and silver and iron; and then he saw just a stone "cut out without hands", a little stone... but it began to grow and develop and it became a mighty universe and it filled the whole world and it smashed the image, all the gold and the silver and the iron and the brass, and there was nothing left (Dan 2:31–35).

What does that mean? It means that the kingdom of the Christ of God is an everlasting kingdom, there will never be an end to it. The Babylonians were great, but they have gone; the kingdoms of Greece were great, but they have vanished; Rome was a mighty empire, she has gone; Egypt was once great, but nothing is left of its glory. Britain, Spain, all these come and go. But there is one kingdom that will never go, it is this glorious kingdom of God. And the day is coming when the kingdoms of this world shall have become the kingdom of our God and of His Christ.

We read in Revelation, "And the devil that deceived them was cast into the lake of fire and brimstone, where the beast and the false prophet are, and shall be tormented day and night for ever and ever" (Rev 20:10). The kingdom shall never be removed. Why not? Because the King is the Son of God who came into this world, and He has already demonstrated His superiority; He has vanquished every enemy. In this world He met every power that could ever be raised against Him and against God, and He mastered, he conquered them all. He cast out devils—yes, He beat the devil himself. He has conquered even the last enemy, which is death. The Resurrection proclaims Him the "Conqueror renowned" who never shall be defeated.

> Jesus shall reign where'er the sun
> Doth his successive journeys run;
> His kingdom stretch from shore to shore,
> Till moons shall wax and wane no more.
>
> Isaac Watts

Do you see the importance of not refusing "Him that speaketh"? Do you want to be shaken to all eternity? Do you want to be in eternal misery and darkness, when this offer is made to you of being in everlasting glory and eternal joy and happiness? Are you in this kingdom of God my friends? If you are you will be very ready to sing this:

> On the Rock of Ages founded,
> What can shake thy sure repose?

Can life shake it? No! Can death shake it? No! Angels, principalities, powers, things present, things to come, nothing can shake your sure repose if you are founded on the Rock of Ages. It is established by God in His Son. People are in it, and belong to the Rock, and nothing can ever shake them, nothing can ever remove them.

> With salvation's walls surrounded,
> Thou may'st smile at all thy foes.

What is the future? Who knows? Is there a war coming? I do not know. All I know is this: Let them do their worst, let hell be let loose, let the devil rage in his last raging, he cannot affect me as a member of the City of God; he cannot touch me as I belong to the "new Jerusalem", which is in heaven and will descend and come down out of heaven.

> Glorious things of thee are spoken,
>   Zion, city of our God!
> He, whose word cannot be broken,
>   Formed thee for His own abode.

My dear friends, have you refused Him that speaketh? See that you refuse Him not. See these reasons for listening to this glorious message of the kingdom. It is God speaking to you, the God who is going to judge you. It is His last offer, it is the only offer, the only way. And oh, what a way it is, what glories it holds before us! Is there anything in life or in this world that is worthy of a second's consideration or comparison with this? Look again at the glories of the kingdom which cannot be moved, which can never be shaken: begin to enjoy its blessings now.

The way is simple...Repent! Acknowledge your sin, acknowledge your failure, your inability; acknowledge your lost estate, that you cannot stand before God. And then believe the Gospel. Believe that Jesus is the Son of God and that He came to be the mediator of a new covenant, that He came to die to save you and to offer you free pardon and forgiveness, a new life and heirship with Himself of the glories of the everlasting kingdom. Oh, that you might see it and look forward to the day when He shall be reigning "from shore to shore" and you will be with Him sharing in the indescribable glory everlasting, basking in the sunshine of His face. "See that ye refuse not him that speaketh" but rather receive Him. "Believe on the Lord Jesus Christ and thou shalt be saved," immediately, and you will be safe forever and forever.